HORSES, HOUNDS
AND OTHER CRITTERS

HORSES, HOUNDS AND OTHER CRITTERS

Humorous Tales of Rural Life

GAYLE BUNNEY

VICTORIA · VANCOUVER · CALGARY

Heritage House Publishing Company Ltd.
heritagehouse.ca

Library and Archives Canada Cataloguing in Publication
Bunney, Gayle, 1954–
    Horses, hounds and other critters: humorous tales of rural life / Gayle Bunney.

(Amazing stories)
Also issued in electronic format.
ISBN 978-1-927051-49-8

    1. Bunney, Gayle, 1954– —Anecdotes. 2. Country life—Alberta—Bonnyville Region—Anecdotes. 3. Farm life—Alberta—Bonnyville Region—Anecdotes. I. Title. II. Series: Amazing stories (Victoria, B.C.)

S522.C3B85 2012   630.97123'3   C2012-901012-X

Series editor: Lesley Reynolds
Proofreader: Liesbeth Leatherbarrow

Cover photo: Makarova Viktoria(Vikarus)/iStockphoto.com

MIX
Paper from
responsible sources
FSC® C016245

The interior of this book was produced on 100% post-consumer recycled paper, processed chlorine free and printed with vegetable-based inks.

Heritage House acknowledges the financial support for its publishing program from the Government of Canada through the Canada Book Fund (CBF), Canada Council for the Arts and the province of British Columbia through the British Columbia Arts Council and the Book Publishing Tax Credit.

Canadian Patrimoine
Heritage canadien

Canada Council   Conseil des Arts
for the Arts   du Canada

BRITISH COLUMBIA
ARTS COUNCIL

16 15 14 13 12   1 2 3 4 5
Printed in Canada

This book is dedicated to the Abrahams,
who are my Bonnyville family:
Bob and Ann, Pandora, Bobby, Leila, Gord and Morria.

Contents

Prologue

IT WAS GOING TO BE ANOTHER one of those hectic days down here on the farm. It had started with fish in my horses' water tank, a baby magpie in my bedroom, a half-dozen wee ankle-biters rolling in the dirt trying to get the smell of skunk off their fur, and now this calamity.

The month-old foal must have lain down next to the fence. When he stood up, he found himself on the wrong side. He was just beginning to get excited about being separated from his momma. This was not good. The gate to get him back on the right side was at the far end of the fenceline. I certainly didn't want him to panic and crash through the wire and injure himself. Since trying to herd a young foal that has not been handled seldom works, I had to catch the unconcerned mare and lead her to the gate to get them reunited.

Of course, the mare had to be the only one I owned that was harder to catch than a good-looking man. The second she saw me with halter in hand, she was off like a witch on a broomstick—and not toward her nervous baby either. He called frantically for his momma, and she just put on more speed heading for the far side of the pasture.

Not to worry, one of my old retired mares was a trusted babysitter for the colt. I haltered her quickly and led her along the fenceline toward the gate, the colt staying fairly calm as he kept pace with us on the other side of the wire fence. Reaching the gate, I eased it wide open for him to come through. His mother had finally figured out that she should come looking for her colt and was coming full throttle.

The colt took a good look at the open gate, dropped to his knees and slipped safely back into the pasture under the bottom wire next to it. That was about the time his momma charged through the gateway before I could even begin to swing it closed. Without slowing down in the slightest, she was soon halfway across the neighbour's field heading for parts unknown.

I closed my eyes and leaned my head against the side of the old mare that was nuzzling the colt like the good baby-sitter that she was. I wondered, "Is it just me or are all my animals abnormal too?"

1

Muk and Luk

GIVE ME STRENGTH TO FORGIVE my grandson Travis for his deeds, for I was innocent until he did an unforgivable thing to me. Everyone knows of my great love for animals. Everyone knows that every two-legged bird, every four-legged animal is dear to my heart. But fish?

In the dead of winter, I wandered out to check my horses' water tank to make sure it was full enough and not frozen over. Lo and behold, there was a cardboard sign duct-taped to it. Upon close inspection of the scribbled writing, I made out the words "Home of Muk and Luk." Wondering who and what in tarnation were a Muk and Luk, I peered into the depths of the water searching for clues. Nothing. Just a stock tank of water and a bottom heater to keep it from freezing solid. But wait—was that a flash of movement under that hot heating coil? Oh, my heavens—a tiny orange goldfish! And look, a tiny black goldfish!

Fish are good. They're good fried, poached and smoked. But I know nothing about live fish. Live fish are good in a beautiful, well-maintained aquarium in someone else's house, not my horse tank.

How those little beggars survived is beyond me. They dared not move out from under that heating coil otherwise hypothermia would have immediately made them slower than molasses in January. And, of course, it was now out of the question to let the horses' tank get almost empty once a month, then take an old straw broom to scrub the algae off the sides and tip out the sludge in order to clean it.

No, now I had to net two little goldfish, put them in a bucket, then scrub and clean their home. Of course, netting them in the green algae sludge was next to impossible. Especially Muk, the black one. What you cannot see, you cannot catch. So I had to take a small bucket and scoop out all the water except for about two inches of solid, green slime. Then I slowly tipped the tank on end and watched for Muk before pouring him out onto the frozen ground, picking him up and putting him in the bucket with his easy-to-see partner, Luk.

Until the last cold snap of the spring, both fish survived under that bare heating coil without getting burned. Thinking spring was here to stay for sure, I unplugged the heating coil as I had spent the winter worrying myself into despair about them touching it. During the night, the tank froze over solid when a cold north wind sprang up. Muk did not survive.

Now what was I going to do? Luk needed a new friend. My usual way of thinking is "bigger is better," and I had heard about some Japanese koi that grew to be humongous, sometimes three feet long or more. Off to the city I went, the word "koi" burned onto my brain. If I was going to have fish, I was going to have huge fish!

I'll continue this story later, when I am off the drugs my doctor prescribed to calm my shattered nerves after buying those "bigger is better" money-devouring, time-consuming monster fish. I also hope I make money on this book so I can quit the second job I need to support them.

CHAPTER

A Horse
of Many Names

AT ONE TIME, MANY MOONS ago, registered horses were few and far between in my main stomping grounds in central Alberta. I generally went to a half-dozen different horse sales each month, held at the livestock auctions in the region. Rocky Mountain House, Innisfail, Rimbey, Ponoka and Stettler had some of the best sales back then. I mostly looked for two- or three-year-old prospects to pick up at a fair price for resale after a couple months of riding. This meant scouting each pen of unknown-ancestry horses with much care before the sale started.

The trick was to look them over real well outside the sale ring, and maybe even watch them being moved from their pen down the alleyway to the ring. This would give me a good idea what I would be in for once I got them home to my own corral. Horses to be avoided were the obvious knot-heads, the roman-nosed ones, the pig-eyed ones, the ones with poor conformation, the crippled ones, the scarred-up ones, the ones with bad feet and the ones who preferred to go over top of you rather than around you.

Once those were passed over, I jotted down the sale number on the rumps of the ones with potential. Because I needed to make a profit after putting some miles on them, I put a question mark beside those that were likely to go higher than I wanted to pay. Those were the ones already halter broke or started and going well under saddle. Someone generally outbid me on them. I would then usually be down to a handful of range horses that hadn't been handled much, if at all. This suited me well, as I always found that if you treated them right, they usually broke out real nice—better, in fact, than many that had been handled wrong by the previous owners.

The sale that day at Cole's Auction Mart was a long one. I had sold one good sorrel gelding about halfway through the sale, which is prime selling time as the bidders are warmed up but haven't spent their available money yet. My gelding worked well for me in the ring, and I was pumped with pride at the price I got for him.

But I still hadn't bought a horse to eat the hay that the gelding would no longer be consuming. One by one, the horses on my list either went too high, or I spotted something

I sold this big thoroughbred mare, Cheetah, at a Rocky Mountain House horse sale as "green broke for an experienced rider only." She bucked me off about 30 seconds after this picture was taken. She was bought by one of Alberta's top guides and outfitters and eventually became one of his toughest saddle horses in the mountains, even though she was never safe for dudes. GAYLE BUNNEY

I didn't like about them once they were in the ring. I swear I could feel my bidding hand start to tremble from lack of use. I was starting to get that "horse-buyers' syndrome" that hits us all sooner or later. You know the one I mean—better to come home with a mule than nothing at all.

And there she was. The last horse into the ring. I had

not seen her out back before the sale, so knew she had been unloaded late. My mind automatically clicked off her good points: pretty head, good conformation—you could see the thoroughbred in her—her feet looked like they were in good shape, and she was wearing a halter with the lead rope looped around her neck.

I waited for the auctioneer to read off her information from the livestock manifest in his hand. His voice boomed out, "Bay mare, broke to ride and pack," and that was it. He went straight to asking for the starting bid. No age? I had only seconds to peg her to be somewhere around eight or nine years old—still young enough that I could ride her a bit and resell her for a profit. A dealer started with a low opening bid; someone to my left in the stands jumped it but only by $50. The dealer standing down in the ring shook his head no instead of giving an answering bid. Going once, going twice, and my bidding hand shot in the air all by itself. The person to my left again jumped the price by $50. My head nodded all by itself for another $50. That horse-buyers' syndrome had struck me full force.

When the dust settled, I'd paid almost as much for the mare as I got for the good gelding I had sold earlier. I couldn't help it though. I was on a roll with my one hand twitching and my head stuck in the nodding up and down position.

I went to load my new prize and had no trouble catching hold of her halter in the pen out back. She bumped me with her head in a friendly greeting. My, she was a nice one.

I stroked her neck and named her Beauty right there on the spot. Before loading her, I made sure that the other buyers loading their horses got a good glimpse of Beauty as I paraded her around. She was a fancy one all right.

Beauty wasn't keen on being loaded, but I took my time, and eventually I was headed for home with her pretty head sticking up over the top of my stock racks. Not that anyone could tell since it was way past midnight before I got her loaded and too dark to spot her in the back of my truck. Once home, I backed up to the bank I used for unloading so a horse could step out easily without jumping down from the truck box.

Well, the sun was coming up before I convinced Silly Girl to step out of that truck so I could put her in a corral with feed and water and go get some shut-eye. Between bumping me with her nose while I was getting her out of the truck and stepping on my toes all the way to the corral, she suited her new name.

I finally got around to putting a saddle on Silly Girl about a week later. She stood quietly while she was saddled. Getting her to take the snaffle bit in her mouth was a bit more hectic. During the process of bridling her, I took a peek at her teeth to confirm her age. Old Girl's dental check placed her somewhere around 15 years old. I hadn't even been close to judging her age accurately back at the horse sale. I didn't think I needed to first mount Old Girl in the round pen at her age, so I led her out to the pasture and swung up.

Well, there was no buck in Dancing Fool, but we jigged to the left and we jigged to the right. Then we danced up the side of a hill that I wasn't aiming on going up. We twirled a couple of pirouettes on top of the hill, then did a two-stepping waltz down the other side. Dancing Fool was enjoying herself greatly, even if I wasn't. By the time I got home, stepped off her and received her customary head-rubbing on my chest to show me how much she liked me, I was a bit tuckered out and dizzy from all the twirling during the final toe-tapping polka coming home.

It took a while before I got to enjoy having an occasional ride on Thumper. The head-butting was getting a bit hard to take. She not only thumped me on the chest now but also thumped me more than once on the side of the head with her hard old noggin. That sometimes brought stars to my eyes and short bursts of language I am not allowed to print here.

I advertised her for sale, but no takers were storming my place to buy a 15-year-old mare that you would have to be more than slightly foolish to buy. I didn't mind though, because if she hadn't sold by the following May, I would introduce her to my new registered thoroughbred stallion and she could just raise me a couple of real nice colts.

May came and went. So did the month of June. July was pretty much over and Hammerhead still wasn't in foal to my stallion. She seemed interested in him some days—interested and friendly until I actually intended for them to get together. Hammerhead then proceeded to kick the living hell out of him, bite chunks out of the post she was tied to and knock me clear across the corral with a direct head thump to whatever part of my anatomy she could throw her head into.

After that, Old Fool just ate grass around the farm and swatted flies in the shade of the spruce trees. Somehow she had convinced me that she was a keeper. I think perhaps one too many blows to my head from hers had rattled me into falling in love with her.

Old Fool must have been about 20 years old when a lady phoned me to see if I knew where she could purchase a quiet old horse to keep her own old mare company. All she wanted was a companion horse so the two of them could live out their lives in peace on her acreage.

She fell in love with that old mare the second she stepped into my horse pasture and laid her hand on her shiny hide. I had warned her about the head butting, but for once, the old mare never tried to butt at all. She just stood there, dozing in the afternoon sun. "She sure is pretty," the lady said as she stroked the mare's nose. The mare rested her head ever-so-gently against the lady's chest. "What's her name?" she asked as she reached for her chequebook. I never hesitated, "Beauty, her name is Beauty."

CHAPTER

3

Which Neighbour's Dog?

I HAD RECENTLY MOVED AND was renting a fine country estate for my horses and me. I was in my glory with a house, corrals, barn and lush green pasture. And cheap rent too! Between working in town, riding colts and taking care of the estate I so happily lived on, I didn't have much time to get to know all my close neighbors, although I often rode by the property of an elderly lady who lived up the road. Her vegetable garden grew right up to the ditch on her property, and I always stopped the colt and said a polite, neighbourly hello while she was busy pulling weeds and packing water to whatever was left after she'd pulled pretty much anything that was green. She was wizened up a bit, kind of like I am now, but she sure was deadly to those weeds. Grumbling and complaining, she would rest on her weed hacker and glare up at me. Even though I was riding in the ditch, my horse seemed to be threatening her well-cared-for patch of weeds—I mean vegetable garden—every time I rode by.

So I kept my conversations fairly short: "Nice day, isn't it? Sure glad we got that rain last week. Trees are sure green this year, aren't they?" or "Sun is sure hot today. Good to see, as it sure helps gardens grow." Then I would nudge the horse with my heels and get out of there.

One day I was riding a snotty five-year-old gelding by her place, not intending to stop, but the old lady raised her hand in friendship for the first time and hailed me. The reason I hadn't intended to stop was that this horse didn't really know the meaning of "whoa" yet, but since she was my neighbour, I spun him in a couple of tight circles and finally got him standing still, darn near on what looked suspiciously like a bedraggled potato plant.

She glared at the horse's front hooves for a second until she saw no damage was done, then said, "I got to dig a grave for an old dog and just don't know if I can do it. Do you think your husband can maybe come over today and give me a hand? Since my own husband passed away, God rest his soul, I find it hard doing such things when they are needed."

My heart went out to the old girl (who was about the age I am now), so I tried to figure out what to say. First, I hadn't seen my hubby since divorce court, which was why I was renting the fine estate next door to her property. Second, if

I didn't get moving pretty quick, this rank gelding was not only going to jump on her potato plant, but maybe on her too. So I said, "Just let me finish miling this horse out on the four-mile circle I do. I should be back in a couple of hours to help you bury the poor old dog. I know what it's like to lose a beloved pet, so I'll be back as soon as possible." She huffed a bit about another woman helping her dig a grave. Just about then, the horse decided it was time to go. I spun him tight and am pretty sure he missed that potato plant with his left back hoof, but I can't swear to that on a bible.

Once home, I cooled the horse out, brushed him and told him about the horse sale that he was going to sooner rather than later. I grabbed a steel bar and a spade, in case she didn't have any, threw them into the back of my truck and headed for her place.

Although her garden was up next to the road, her house was set quite far back, which was why I'd never seen the old dog with her. Poor old thing. I had been hoping for a small-breed dog because digging graves can be hard work. No chance. Wrapped in a blanket that had seen better days and which was tied with baling twine, the deceased looked to be a fairly good-sized dog. My neighbour pointed out a spot at the far end of her yard, and I set into digging. I was young then, so things went fairly well, except the old girl kept telling me to go deeper. Wanting to please, I kept going until she got to thinking that her supper was in the oven and should be ready to eat, so maybe I should just finish the job.

I lifted the carefully and lovingly wrapped deceased and carried it gently to my freshly dug grave. It was all I could do to carry it myself, as I figure that poor old dog weighed a good 80 pounds. Through a small hole in the blanket, I saw shiny black fur protruding. I finished filling in the grave, smoothed the surface exactly as she told me to and hoped she was going to ask me for supper, as I was feeling a bit hungry from the day's work.

I watched her retreat into her house after she told me not to let my horses come so close to her prized vegetable garden again or I would pay the consequences if they harmed it. My rear dragging a bit from exhaustion, I threw my tools into the truck and went home.

A couple of days later, I had booked time off from my town job to work on the fine estate I had rented. I fought with the plumbing in the house until I could flush water without mopping, pounded in some decent posts for the corrals and was starting on the barn, hoping to make it safe to use someday, when another neighbour pulled into my yard.

It appeared that his dog had gone missing three days ago. Had I seen it? He was just a big black mutt, but he kept the coyotes away from the yard. He knew that his dog sometimes bothered the neighbours' livestock, which had some people up in arms. He was hoping I had seen the dog as he worried that the "super-cranky old woman" up the road might have done something to it since she claimed it had once harassed her chickens.

I pounded in another spike and thought about the fact that not once had the old girl said the dog's name or carried on about the loss of a dear old pet. Tapping in the next spike, I then hammered it home. Turning, I said, "I wish I could help you, but I truthfully never saw a black dog running around anywhere near here. But since you stopped, can I get you a cup of coffee or tea? And I have some awesome leftover stew from the other night that will sure fill you up if you're hungry."

Because that's what country neighbours do. They always offer food and drink to someone who stops in.

CHAPTER

4

Bar Hounds

NOWADAYS, RAISING AND SELLING the select offspring of my popular small-breed dogs and working with horses keeps me busy enough that I actually make money working at home most days. While cuddling newborn pups in the quiet of a summer evening, I have time to reflect on my younger days when I not only worked horses for a living but also worked in town to earn money to feed and care for those very same horses that maybe made me a profit on sale day.

I am an executive chef de cuisine by trade, but often found myself doing far more than flipping T-bone steaks on a glowing hot charcoal broiler at just the right moment to ensure they would be blue-rare on the inside but charred nicely on the outside. While working at a hotel, I was designated assistant manager of the entire place when the owner/manager decided to take his customary days off each week.

Cooking was more my style. I went to work, changed into my white chef's uniform and even put on that crazy piece of flop-happy headgear called a chef's hat when I absolutely had too. I looked pretty professional, even if you did glance downward and see the toes of my cowboy boots sticking out from under the starched white hem of my uniform trousers.

When lounge or dining-room waitresses failed to show up for their shift, back in my office I would change into the inn's designated white blouse and black skirt, mumbling as I gently set my cowboy boots to one side, pulled on nylons and slipped my feet into much-hated ladies' dress shoes. Then I tried to remember to smile, smile, smile. Either because of my smile or the fact that I was sleek and trim-looking back then, I sometimes made enough in tips to buy several bags of oats for those horses eating me out of house and home. I just smiled and smiled. I couldn't really walk well in those shoes, but I stayed happy over those tips—except for when a certain customer pinched my rear once too often one night. I suspect his black eye healed up just fine after a week or two.

The Saturday-night bar scene was another story entirely. I was allowed to wear my blue jeans, providing they were a newer pair without the customary worn or ripped patches that most of my jeans eventually featured. I always wore my newest shirt and shined my boots real nice. I stuck with the bronzed quarter-horse belt buckle I was so proud of, nothing too fancy. Back then I filled my jeans out as best I could, since I didn't have many curves, mostly just strong legs and arms from training colts.

The regular bar staff liked having me around because I knew how to work. I got along well with the bar patrons too, as it was a country bar with western music, and I knew a lot of those Saturday-night folks. Heck, I remember my tips for just one weekend paid for almost a half-ton load of square bales. Horses eat a lot, you know!

I was a busy person, but one day I had a spare moment to sit down to chat with one of my staff. I was feeling blue because my then one-and-only dog on the farm had passed away. I was determined not to get another dog until I had more time to spend with him, and with this town job, spare time was only a figment of my imagination.

The staff got together and had a little party for me on a slow Monday night. I could see the box all wrapped up nicely and was hoping for those new riding boots called Ropers because I liked the look of them, even if they did have laces that would take a month of Sundays to do up. Finally, with much cheering, I was handed the box. I behaved myself and gently removed the wrapping paper instead of ripping it off like a rabid dog. I reached in my hip pocket, dug out my jackknife, cut through layers of tape and went to take a look, hoping to see a new pair of fancy cowgirl boots.

And there he was, remote control included. The cutest dang mechanical dog you ever saw! I didn't have to feed this one—he was battery operated. With that remote, you could make him go forward and sometimes backwards and bark his fool head off. He was about eight inches high, and if you closed your eyes and thought about it, almost realistic. Everyone sat there, beer in hand, and waited for my reaction.

With a tear in my eye, and being the good sport that I am, I thanked everyone and named that pup Grizzly due to his colour. Somehow Grizzly ended up kept on a low shelf behind the bar, next to the extra Clamato juice and napkins that we always seemed to run short of. Maybe I put him there to protect the napkins, I just don't remember. We occasionally had a lot of fun entertaining the customers with Grizzly on slow nights.

One particular Saturday night, I was not in a good mood. A couple of days before, I had been dumped, and dumped hard, by a colt I was working with. I was stiff and sore. Second, I hadn't had a day off from this town job of mine for well over a month. I was a hurting puppy and tired to boot. Third, the hotel's owner/manager knew I was tired and sore but dared tell me that even though I had opened the restaurant at 5:00 a.m. and worked all day, he was having company that evening so I would have to manage the bar all night. And worse, both of the bar's night bouncers had quit without notice. I would be on my own, with no backup. I told myself that this was going to be the last time. My winter's feed was bought and paid for. I had colts to ride and sell before people quit buying horses with the savage cold soon coming. Only one more time!

You have to picture the scene with your eyes closed to get the true meaning of it. There were the regular patrons, town and country folk, but also on that night a whole bunch of young hellion cowboys who considered this particular bar to be their home stomping grounds. Then there were the equally young and strong oil-rig workers who just happened to get the night off and showed up for a good time. They were strangers to this particular bar, but no strangers to hell-raising fun at any bar near where they were working.

At first these out-for-a-good-time oil-rig workers just played pool and danced to the band's loud music without much fuss. The trouble was they were short on good-looking female dance partners—and the best-looking young ladies happened to be sitting with the cowboys. With no bar bouncers, I was just working the floor and trying to keep things under control. I wasn't much for size back then, but I had the smarts to keep smiling and stop most of the ruckus before it got out of hand. The cowboy crowd was doing pretty well, even letting their ladies dance with the out-of-town workers until one cowboy's good-looking girlfriend exchanged what looked suspiciously like a kiss with her husky new dancing partner. The trouble hit the fan in a blink of an eye.

Nowadays, you take the fight outside to the parking lot. Back then, tables and chairs got thrown left, right and centre until a good fighting space was available. The band quit and started worrying about moving their guitars to a safer location. I was tired. I was real tired. I was mega sore. I was lacking sleep and in no mood for what was about to happen. The pushing and the loud threats were unnerving me big time. I stood there, all of five feet four inches tall, and tried to talk sense into those redneck boys. Soon an arena was cleared for fighting in the middle of the bar. I patrolled up and down as threats were thrown and the bad language escalated. The girl behind the bar was waiting for my signal to dial the police, her hand trembling over the phone and her face as white as a sheet.

Then I felt it—the remote for Grizzly in my shirt pocket. He was in position. I had taken him down off the shelf in order to bring up more napkins. Could he do it? I put pressure on the "go" button and played with the remote. Then I hit the "arf, arf, arf" centre button. Out Grizzly came, barking his fool head off and little legs just a scrabbling. I quit playing with his buttons when he was dead centre between the local cowboys and the visiting good-timers. In my meanest, no-nonsense voice, I explained how Grizzly could tear a man's leg off in one bite. Not a man moved, not a sound was heard. Sound and motion were suspended. I fiddled some more and Grizzly gave his warning bark, just as he ran into the far wall and kept trying to go forward, even though I was pressing hard on his reverse lever.

It worked. Every single fighting madman on both sides began to laugh. Instead of throwing punches, they slapped each other on the back and ordered rounds of drinks for each other as shouts of good cheer erupted. Grizzly's job was done.

I eventually gave Grizzly to a little boy who fell in love with him when visiting my farm. To this day, that was perhaps the best little bar hound I ever owned!

CHAPTER

Studley

ONE JULY, I RECEIVED A PHONE CALL from a lady who had seen me selling and buying horses at the auction sales in Rocky Mountain House, Ponoka, Stettler and Innisfail. She was impressed with the fact I was about the only woman doing so way back then. She also was impressed with the fact that I was gentle with my horses instead of cowboying them with spurs, etc., to get a good performance in the sale ring.

When I was selling horses that I'd had plenty of rides on, I rode them first with a saddle, then jumped off, quickly removed the saddle and bridle and continued to work them bareback with just a halter. I could slide off their rumps and hang onto their tails as they pulled me around and even crawl between their hind legs. This made the lady pretty sure I was one special horse trainer.

Now me being me, by the time she finished telling me all this, my head was swollen up with pride to twice its normal size. Standing there on the phone, my chest grew about 10 inches as it swelled with that old "I am the best" attitude I was occasionally known for. At this rate, I was going to have to invest in a new cowboy hat and bigger shirts to fit my suddenly enlarged body parts. Pride will do that to a person.

Finally the lady got down to telling me the reason she was phoning me. It seemed she had a real nice horse that she just had to sell and sell now. I may have been a bit stuck on myself from the first part of the phone call, but I am also a fairly careful horse buyer, which means I don't want to pay more than the horse is worth. In fact, paying less than what it's worth is pretty good too. I was instantly in horse-buying mode, which is somewhere between "Sorry, you want too much money" and "Bring him on out to my place, as I am sure I will like him."

The conversation went like this. Lady: "He is only a four-year-old and so sweet."

Me: "How much riding has he had?"

Lady: "Get this—when he was only a yearling, we would put the saddle on him, bridle him and lead him all over with our border collie sitting on the saddle, as of course he was much too young for us to put our weight on his back and ride him. Our dog would be walking all over the top of that horse and barking, and the horse just loved that dog. He is such a pet that we often let him just graze the lawn next to the house. He was like having another dog around; he is such a sweetie."

Me: "So, it sounds like he is pretty gentle. He must be pretty well broke now as a four-year-old."

Lady: "Both my husband and I work, and we only had time to ride him a few times when he was a two-year-old. He was the most perfect horse to ride. Never bucked or reared or tried to run away. He just loved all the extra attention he was getting when we rode him."

Me: "So how much riding has he had in the last two years?"

Lady: "Well, once my husband's shoulder got injured, he really wasn't ridden anymore. I mean, I know how to feed, water him and stuff like that, but I'm not really very experienced with horses. So you see, it's only my husband who knows how to ride. My husband's shoulder seemed to stiffen up after the injury and he couldn't ride then, which is sad because our horse loved to be ridden."

I was thinking that even if not ridden for the last couple of years, such a good horse had already proven that he had a good disposition, and it would be very easy to advance his training. I could easily make him into a good, honest horse that would excel for any rider. Heck, he sounded perfect!

Me: "You would have to deliver him to my place as I have too many horses on the go right now to spend time on the road picking up another one. So what are you asking for him, including delivery?"

The lady proceeded to quote me a very decent, in fact, really low price for the horse but said they did not own a horse trailer or stock racks for the back of their truck, so delivery was out of the question. I knew of a man in her area who often hauled livestock for other people in his old, beat-up, homemade trailer, pulled by a truck that was mostly rusted out but always seemed to get from point A to point B. The guy did it mostly for beer money, so it was the cheapest way to get the horse delivered. I told her about him, and she confirmed she knew of him around their small town. She said she would phone him about delivering the horse, but would need payment up front for him.

Now before I paid up front for a horse that I had never laid eyes on, I needed to ask a whole bunch more questions, like, "What breed is he?" She said his sire had thoroughbred in him, and his dam was a stout, chunky "kind of draft-horse-looking mare." Now this was back in the days when the registered quarter horses that are now so popular were few and far between here in Canada. On top of that, I knew that a thoroughbred with some draft in him made the best many-hard-miles-a-day, ranch-type horse and the best mountain horse, in my opinion. Big, tough horses. My next question was, "How many hands tall is he?" The lady had no clue what I meant by hands tall, so I explained. "Okay, I am five feet four inches tall, so that makes me exactly 16 hands tall." I had found numerous times that this was the best way to explain to someone how tall their horse was. I then explained that a horse is measured from the top of their withers straight down to the ground. So how tall was she and where were his withers compared to the top of her head?

Excited now, she said, "Oh, I am five feet five inches tall, and his withers are equal with the top of my head when I stand beside him."

That sounded about right for this type of crossbreed, which would be about 16.1 hands tall. It was a nice size, as ranchers running cattle on huge tracts of land, the cowboys who worked for them, and mountain outfitters did not like to ride small horses. I then asked what colour he was, since that seems to be important to many people, even though I always thought a good horse was a good horse regardless of the colour. She said he was the most beautiful black horse in the country.

I was getting hooked like a fish on the way to the frying pan. I do like black horses, and apparently other people like them too, as I've found they resell quickly. I asked my last few questions: "Now he's not lame or anything, is he? He doesn't have anything wrong with him, right? No breathing problems such as heaves? No founder in his hooves? His hooves aren't cracked up, down or sideways? No bad scars? No lumps, bumps or anything like that on his legs or anywhere on his body?"

She sighed and said, "He is beautiful and there is nothing wrong with him. It's just that my husband and I admire you so much when we see you at the horse auctions. We know he needs more training and we want someone like you to be the one to do that training. We want him to get better broke, and we want that to be done gently like we know you do."

My pride exploded again, and I am sure a couple of buttons popped off my shirt from my chest swelling. I told her to contact the man who made extra money hauling livestock, then changed my mind and said, "Heck, I'll contact him myself." We said goodbye and I went out to finish horse chores, which never seem to end. I thought about this black gelding and his size and the fact he sounded like a sweetheart and would be easy to finish training. No doubt I could make a reasonable profit off him with just 30 to 60 days more riding. I would be missing the best time of year to sell horses by the time he was ready for sale, but he sounded like the type that would sell well even later in the fall months.

I had supper, and then sat down to give the horse hauler a phone call. He jumped at the chance to make a bit more beer money and said he had to haul to my area in the next week. Since he was already coming, he quoted me a really good price to load the horse on his trailer and deliver it at the same time. I asked if he had enough cash on him to pay for the horse, and I would pay him back when he got to my place. He thought about that for a while and then agreed.

I gave him the seller's phone number and said, "See you soon." I was one happy camper. I didn't have to hit the road and drive a long way, plus the deal was just too good to pass up. After all, making money with horses was tough enough without wasting time on the road, which took time away from riding the colts I already had at home.

Well, the hauler's one or two weeks turned into over a month before he finally showed up. His beat-up truck chugged into my yard with his decrepit homemade horse trailer attached to the bumper. I was just unsaddling a colt, so finished doing that before I went to greet him. The beer fumes pouring off him showed that he was well on his way to being tipsy, and I hadn't even paid him yet. I no sooner had time to shake his hand than a loud bang came from his trailer. After a couple more loud bangs, I saw one board come loose and dangle there on the right-hand side of that trailer. I caught a flash of the hoof doing the damage. The trailer started rocking and almost jumped off the rusted axles. I heard snorting and blowing and started to have a sinking feeling in my chest. Then, of all things, I heard the distinctive woof of an angry sow pig. The pig sounded like it was more upset than the horse.

Now, horses that have never seen pigs before can be scared to death of them. And this man had a pig and a horse in the same narrow, two-horse trailer. We stood behind it and watched chunks of its right side go flying as that horse kicked sideways. I was getting upset, as I knew this old guy knew that horses were often afraid of pigs. I asked him what he was pulling off here, as the horse was obviously in distress over being hauled with a pig. He scratched at his week's worth of pathetic beard and said, "Nope that horse is used to pigs. They had pigs too. That horse is wrecking my trailer and has been wrecking it since I left their place to deliver him to you. In fact, unless you have some planks here to fix the side of my trailer, I am going to have to charge you more."

I choked on that statement and said, "Well let's get him unloaded."

"Sure thing," he said. "The sooner the better, unless you want to fix the entire right side of my trailer." He opened the tailgate and swung it wide. On the left side of the trailer divider was one angry pregnant sow on her way to a new home to have babies, and on the right was Studley.

I didn't have to worry about untying him, as he flew backwards, breaking the lead rope, and landed about a foot in front of my nose. He scrambled to his feet and turned to face me—all 14 hands of him. He was barely over pony size! He sniffed my jacket, stomped a front foot and whirled around toward my horses in the corrals. He squealed, he squalled and lit out on a dead run towards them. He literally slammed into the fence trying to get in a pen where I had a mare I was training for a customer.

This was not a gelding, this was a stallion! Oh my heavens—my mind went back to the lady's phone call.

Studley

I had never asked if he was gelded, and I had no one to blame but myself. This horse was a raging, out-of-control, testosterone-driven stallion. I quickly opened a gate, and as he charged up and down the fenceline, he ran through it. I was able to trap him in another pen away from the mare that was attracting him big time.

The horse hauler was busy writing on his cigarette package with a pencil, figuring out the damage to his trailer to add to what I already owed him. That sow was getting madder by the minute and thinking about getting out of the trailer. Mrs. Pig wasn't much smaller than the horse he had just delivered. When he was done figuring, he turned to me with the total cost of delivering Studley and paying for him, as I had asked him to do.

I did have a pile of good lumber, and he agreed to take enough to build an entire new homemade trailer. I asked if he'd had any problems loading the stud. He replied, "That bugger tore the shoulder muscles out of the husband last year with his teeth. Poor guy is crippled now from that stud bite. They made a pet out of him, but then he wouldn't stay home, kept jumping their fences to get in with the neighbour's mares. The neighbour didn't mind as he got free colts. He was hard to load until I put one of the neighbour's mares in first on the left side, and then he loaded no problem. Then I just had to unload the mare. Oh, by the way, I picked up the sow afterwards."

He went on to rant about how hard it was to load a sow

when it had never seen a horse before. He wanted to be paid and paid now, but I had one more question for him. I said, "You have known me for a long, long time and you know I deal only with big, stout horses. Did you not think this horse was a bit too small for my liking?"

He coughed up some cigarette smoke and said, "Yup, figured that one out too. You told her you were 16 hands tall and reached the top of a horse's withers. She figured a horse's withers was the top of his head and be danged, if she wasn't right—his ears are a bit over 16 hands tall."

I paid him while gritting my teeth in an unladylike fashion, and he rattled away. The corral Studley was in had no feed or water, so I got a water barrel and brought the garden hose to fill it. He came up to the fence to see me, like a playful puppy, then pinned his ears back and tried to take a chunk out of me over the top rail. I then threw some hay into his corral and leaned on the fence to take a close look at the stud pony. As sure as water don't run uphill, I was going to lose money on this horse and maybe some of my hide too. As I was leaning there, Studley whipped his head around from the pile of hay I had given him and, ears back and teeth bared, charged me on the other side of the fence.

It was no use phoning the lady, as she hadn't really lied to me. She just didn't tell me the whole truth. I phoned a neighbour who was an excellent horseman and who had often helped me out when I needed a second pair of hands. His wife called him to the phone, and I got right down to business. I needed some help getting the trip ropes on a stud to lay him down and castrate him. The sooner the better, as the best way to change his behaviour was to change his raging testosterone-driven attitude. He said he could pop over the next night after supper. Then he chuckled and asked me why I had a stallion on the place anyway since I wasn't breeding horses now, just training them. I mumbled something about not passing up a good deal and left it at that.

By the next evening, Studley had settled down a bit, especially once I got a stud chain on him. He was learning that biting wasn't such a good idea. Oh, he still tried about every two minutes, but he was learning. The operation went smoothly, although when we let him up he managed to tear the neighbour's shirt with his teeth, missing human flesh by a hair. He then rapidly backed up toward both of us and let fly with both hind feet. The neighbour stepped to the left, I stepped to the right and Studley's flying heels missed both of us. He had some big lessons to learn in life, including that he wouldn't be spoiled any more or allowed to be a danger to anyone and everyone.

I would leave him in the corral for a few days to heal up, then put him out on pasture for a couple of months with some tough older draft geldings about three times his size that wouldn't tolerate his bad-dude attitude They would do a fine job of educating him. By then, I would be riding him in the cold, but it takes a while for a new gelding to settle down, especially when he's bred mares as a stud and got away with misbehaving with humans. I would never get him sold before next year, but heck, he wasn't very big so wouldn't eat that much hay over the winter. Maybe I would even make enough money off him to pay for the hay. There was no use dreaming about making a profit, as that was never going to happen. I doubted he would ever be safe for kids or ladies, and at his diminutive size, that was who he was suited for.

A couple of days later, the phone rang early in the morning. I had barely started on my first cup of coffee for the day, which meant I didn't have enough caffeine in my system yet to be really on the ball. I answered it and heard a deep voice ask me if I was the lady who had bought the black stud a few days ago. I confirmed that I was. He said he was the sellers' neighbour and had some fine-looking colts off that stud. In fact, those colts had been spoken for by buyers while still nursing their mammas. For top dollar too. I grunted some reply to him and took another sip of caffeine. His next sentence wrecked my day; in fact, it wrecked my whole week and most of the rest of the month too.

He proceeded to offer me five times what I had paid for Studley. I never make that kind of profit buying, training and then reselling the best of horses. The cash register in my head was going ka-ching, ka-ching. My hands started to tremble at the thought of all that money, making the coffee in my cup slosh all over the floor. I stared at the puddle, and my voice came out in a high-pitched squeak, "You don't mind if he is gelded, do you?"

44

Studley

The deep voice on the phone got even deeper, kind of like a growling dog, "That black is one of only three registered quarter-horse studs that I know about in this province with that good of a pedigree. Of course I don't want you to geld him first. I didn't even know they were going to sell him or I would have bought him in a second."

I couldn't even talk, but I am guessing that my silence spoke louder than any words I might have said. "No," he said, "please tell me no. You haven't already gelded him?"

My voice cracking with emotion, I replied, "Studley is no longer Studley; he is well, an ex-Studley now. But you can have him for what I paid for him, if that helps any." Now it was his turn to be speechless. A second later, I heard the click as he hung up the phone.

And me? I went back to bed and stayed there hidden under the covers for most of the day. Hiding my head under the covers helped to stop the now-broken cash register in my head from going ka-ching.

CHAPTER

Rented Barns

THE THING ABOUT BEING a single cowgirl with a touch of wanderlust running through your veins is you never seem to stay put for very long. There is always another piece of this big country to live in and new people and new places to make each day a challenge. Horses have always gone with me on each move, so there were barns of all shapes and sizes on most pieces of property I rented. The house never mattered much to me, but shelter for the horses was a must.

Some years ago, a widow lady answered my ad in the regional newspaper looking for pasture, shelter and corrals along with a house to rent in her area. I had already found employment there to make extra money on the side, with enough time off to do my training and riding.

The house was no screaming hell. Quite a while back she
had moved out of it into a mobile home she had put on her
property. I figured as long as I kept the wood stove smoking
hot, I would be able to keep next winter's freezing winds at
bay, and a few mousetraps would take care of whatever my
blue heeler dog couldn't catch. The pasture fences weren't in
the best of shape, nor were the corrals, which had sat empty
for years, but I was used to fixing and repairing daily at
most places I rented, so I could handle that too.

But the barn was to die for. It sat there in all its glory,
looking brand spanking new, as if it had never been used.
The lady's husband had put fine craftsmanship into that
barn just before he suddenly passed away. There were
three first-rate stalls for horses or calving cows and a well-
designed tack or storage room. The wood inside that barn
gleamed as if it had been hand polished. A straw broom and
a big old metal dustpan leaned against the alley wall. Not a
cobweb was to be seen. I was sure I could put this splendid
barn to good use.

But there was a problem. That widow lady fussed
something awful about me abusing that barn from the
second I moved onto the property. While I was storing
my saddles and equipment in the tack room, she hovered
over me making a kind of "tut tut" sound low in her throat.
When I was finished hauling stuff inside, I meandered on
outside and made mistake number one—I didn't close the
door to the tack room when I left. She not only closed it, but

that low-sounding "tut tut" became a steady "tisk, tisk, tisk" in a somewhat higher octave.

Mistake number two happened soon after. I hauled a half-ton load of fresh-cut, sweet-smelling, square alfalfa bales home. I was going to be training someone's horse to make some extra revenue, and the bales were a down payment on my fees. The widow lady wasn't at home when I carried them in and stacked them in the first stall on the left. It was a perfect place for them, protected from the rain and snow. I not only left the stall door open to ensure the bales could breathe a bit and not go mouldy, but I also left the exterior barn door open so air could circulate for a couple of days for the same reason. Then I chased a fat mouse out of the house bathroom into the waiting jaws of my blue heeler, took a quick shower and headed off to my town job.

It was plumb dark when I wearily drove into the yard that night. Even so, as my truck headlights flashed on it on the way to the house, I knew I had done wrong with that barn again. The door was closed tight as a drum. I began to suspect that the widow lady had a thing about doors being left open.

Sure enough, the next morning I strolled down to the barn and walked inside to find the stall door shut tight too. And there was something else—the bits of hay that had fallen on the floor were gone, swept up so not a trace remained. I glanced around and saw that every single strand of fallen hay had been carefully placed in a large cardboard box in the corner with the crudely printed words "Please Use For Garbage" written on the side. I now strongly suspected that I had a door-closing, clean-barn freak on my hands.

It took a couple of weeks of hard labour to get the last new posts dug in and new planks up on one of the corrals so I could use it for starting colts. I had no need to take a horse near the barn, as I simply packed my saddle and other tack down to the corral and whatever wild-eyed young horse awaited me. Every day when I was finished, before dragging my often weary butt up to the house, I did a mental check that I had closed all doors and swept up any mud or dirt that fell off my boots. The best part about getting to the house was making sure that dog of mine was revved up into kill mode before I threw open the creaky old door. In he would charge, nails clawing on the old linoleum for traction as he nailed the mouse closest to the door. On a good day, he could get another one before they all disappeared into holes in the wall. I figured in another few months, between the traps and the dog, I should have the mouse population down to maybe only a couple of hundred. Life was good.

My third barn mistake was a doozy in the widow lady's book on barns. By now, I had a mental checklist: close all doors, sweep the floor as I backed out of the barn each night and knock down any cobwebs that were also apparently my fault when they appeared. I had all that down pat, but on this particular day, I committed the ultimate sin. Or, to be exact, one of the horses did.

I had worked a colt for a few miles, and everything was going well until I was close to home. That was when the bluest of prairie skies suddenly darkened. Within minutes, a late fall thundershower beat down on us. Both the horse and I were soaked in seconds. When I got back to the yard, I never thought twice about throwing open that barn door and leading the horse in to unsaddle him out of the downpour before I led him to the pasture gate and turned him loose. Then I went back to the barn for my end-of-the-day ritual of door closing and cleaning. And there it sat, right in the middle of that barn floor! That silly horse had lifted his tail and left his mark! Using a pitchfork, I threw most of the pile out the door. Then I swept and swept some more until only a damp yellow stain remained. I figured once the wood dried I would be home free. Sadly, it was not to be.

The next day I was working a morning shift in town so didn't go near the barn until late afternoon. First, I called the horses into the corral with a bite of grain, then I walked over to the barn, opened the door and walked in to get my saddle. The smell of disinfectant was sharp and clear. That spot on the floor had been scrubbed so thoroughly that I swear the widow lady had caused a slight hollow by scrubbing some of the wood away. In a neat line she'd carefully placed the cardboard garbage box, the straw broom, the metal dustpan, a mop, a mop bucket and, last but not least, a can of disinfectant. Taped on the front of that can was a scribbled sign that read, "Please Use Daily."

I had intended to put horses in the stalls in that barn during the cold of winter, but how could I dare to leave a horse in there overnight? The thought of the amount of cleaning that would have to be done was simply too frightening for me to handle. It looked like it was time for me to find another place to live. Besides, my old dog wasn't having much fun anymore. It seemed like the house was running out of mice, and he was pining away with nothing much left for excitement. He needed the challenge of new surroundings as much as I did.

CHAPTER

7

Panty Hose and Playing Dress-Up

CONTRARY TO POPULAR BELIEF, the life of a cowgirl is not all fun and games. True, we have more than our fair share of hilarious happenings, but there always seems to come a day when not everything goes right, as I am so fond of pointing out to people.

The one thing that can wreck my entire day is having to go to a wedding or some other fancy function. True, the food is almost always great, and the wine usually flows freely for those who wish to partake in a glass or two. For the most part, the people are friendly, and you wish you could hug them all close to your breast—although it sometimes requires an extra glass of wine to put yourself in a huggy kind of mood.

So why did the upcoming wedding of a dear friend of mine put me on edge? Well, I might as well just blurt this out and get it over with: I hate playing dress-up! When Gary (my former husband) and I were married, I wore my favourite cowboy boots and cowboy hat because we were married on horseback and I could get away with it. It was the best wedding I ever went to. I say that not because it was my wedding, but because I didn't have to trip along in a dress and high heels. That and having the entire wedding party include some of the nicest horses in the country made it a special event.

Sadly, my friend's wedding was to be a fancy affair without a horse in sight. Since I didn't own a recent gala-event dress or the footwear to go along with such a dress, my first job would be to go shopping, but in a ladies' wear store instead of my usual western clothing store. I steeled myself to the task, determined that this time I would find the right fancy wear all in one store and not have to go to 20 of them like I'd done before when faced with the same problem.

I managed to postpone getting the dress-up stuff until just a couple of days before the big event. I chose a city store that promised anything and everything in one-stop shopping. The saleslady who helped me with my search thought I was joking when I said I didn't know what size of dress I needed. Fourteen dresses later, I settled on a pale blue, puffy-looking one that the saleslady assured me went well with my windblown complexion and chunky build. The shoes were next. I knew I took a boys' size six wide in riding boots, but that didn't seem to help the saleslady figure out my ladies' shoe size.

Twenty-some pairs later, I settled on a decent pair with three-inch heels that were sturdy enough so I wouldn't tip over too often. The store looked like a cyclone had hit it. With dresses lying around and shoes scattered from north to south, the saleslady seemed a bit stressed and glad I was almost done.

I was set to depart when it hit me that my cotton socks that nestled so well in my boots would not be appropriate for this particular dress and shoes. Not wanting to stress the poor dear any further with more questions, I grabbed a couple of pairs of neutral-coloured pantyhose and paid for my purchases. I eased past the scattered shoes and empty shoe boxes and headed out the door for home.

The day of the wedding arrived much too quickly for my taste, but I was as ready as I would ever be. I had borrowed a friend's car to drive to the wedding rather than ride in my beat-up old pickup truck, which smelled rather strongly of horses, cows and dogs. I showered, shampooed and shaved the hair off my usually hidden lower limbs. I dressed with the utmost care. Stepping back from my floor-length mirror, I had to admit I looked good—real good in fact. Maybe this getting dressed up once in a while wasn't such a bad idea after all. Looking so dang pretty and all, I was sure to turn a few heads.

I jumped into that cute little car, revved the engine and headed out. Now, being a horse owner, I checked my watch to make sure I had time to swing south for a few miles and check the horses I had on rented pasture for the summer. All I needed to do was slow down when I went by the pasture, count them and make sure all were up and moving around. I slowed as I reached the open field and quickly counted— all up and grazing peacefully. I was starting to pick up speed again when the gate from their pasture out onto the road came into view. It was wide open.

I hit the brakes and parked the car. I had asked the farmer I was renting from if I could padlock the gate to prevent anyone from opening it, and he had said no, as he might want to take machinery across the land during harvest. He had assured me that if he did, he would close the gate as soon as he passed through it. Well, someone had left it wide open. Thank heavens the horses hadn't come across it yet.

I jumped out of the car in a hurry to close the gate and ended up stumbling through tall grass that snagged the heels on my new ladies' shoes. That just doesn't happen with riding boots. A mild mumbling escaped my lips, all done up with their pretty lipstick. I grabbed the fallen gate, pulled it tight and slipped the bottom into its loop of wire. Where in tarnation was the top loop of wire to secure the gate closed? I looked around. It wasn't on the post or lying on the ground.

This was when I came to the conclusion that driving one's own vehicle is a must, wedding or not. Behind the seat in my beat-up old truck were wire, rope and fencing pliers—everything a person could ever need in a situation like this. I glanced at my borrowed car. It sat there void of all necessary fencing materials, looking smug in its cleanliness.

If there is one thing I know about myself, it's that I am a very resourceful person. I always seem to find a way to muddle through emergencies. So I glanced down. Nope, my fancy shoes did not have boot laces that could be used to tie this gate closed. Peeking out of the top of those shoes was my only hope: my pantyhose.

If I hurried, I could use them to tie the gate closed and rush home for the other pair I had bought. I could still make it to the wedding on time. I took a quick glance up and down the road. No vehicles coming to see my partial striptease. With a bit of squirming I had that pair of hose off in no time flat. After two quick wraps around the gate post, my horses were once again confined. The wire ripped the pantyhose instantly, but the deed was done.

The little car spun a donut, and I roared for home. I took the steps into the house two at a time, ladies' shoes or no ladies' shoes. The clock was ticking loudly, and time was running out. I ripped the hose package open and commenced to shake the folded nylon out into the shape of pantyhose. With two shakes, I knew I was in trouble. While the first pair had fit like a dream, I was mighty doubtful about this pair. They looked to be several feet long and several feet wide. Wouldn't you know it, pantyhose came in more than one size! I held them aside and glanced down at my lily-white legs that never saw the sun. I sure couldn't go to this fancy-dress affair with those bare legs. Mumbling loudly to myself, I pulled on the oversized hose. I tucked the elasticized top up and under my armpits, and it seemed to work.

I made it to the wedding on time, but only because it started a good half-hour late. The bride was beautiful and the groom as handsome as a pedigree stallion. The food, drinks and dancing that followed were accompanied with laughter from the crowd of happy guests. I suppose some people thought it odd that I kept my arms clasped tightly to my sides, but I had to. It was the only way to keep those one-piece nylons tucked up there in my armpits to prevent severe, unsightly sagging at the ankles. It limited my ability to do a lot of up-close hugging too. I sure hope they didn't think I was being unfriendly.

CHAPTER

Green Dogs, Children and Horse Toads

OUR CHILDREN ARE VERY SPECIAL to us. They come in all shapes, sizes and ancestry. My favourites are the little ones who only come to about their parents' waists—little folk with minds of their own already. Proud mommas and poppas often try very hard to please them and give them what they are asking for. Sometimes the little guys and gals get what they so adamantly desire and sometimes they don't.

One day a young couple came to buy a puppy from one of my wee dog's litters. I had barely finished mowing my out-of-control lawn grass when they arrived. They trooped into my house, their equally wee girl in tow—a sweetheart if ever I saw one. Daintily she examined each of the five puppies. As she gently inspected them, I marvelled at how careful she was. Her proud parents informed me that their cat had given birth to kittens earlier that year, and their wee munchkin had learned to be ever so nice with the kittens. Because they had given all the kittens away, they had promised her a puppy of her very own. She was to decide which one would go home with them.

Carefully she set them all in a row. Reaching down she picked up what seemed to be her final choice—a tri-coloured boy puppy that busied himself licking her fingers and wagging his plume of a feathered tail. She stood up, clutching the puppy to her chest with love in her eyes. The munchkin turned towards her adoring parents, but before she could say anything, she glanced down at the dog that came barrelling in through the dog door from outside. A totally green dog, bright and vivid grass green. She gasped and almost dropped the puppy in her arms. Sensing disaster, I quickly moved in to catch the pup should she drop it. She let the puppy slip into my hands without even thinking about it.

"That one, Mommy and Daddy, that green one right there is the one I want!" Horrified parental eyes turned toward what was once one of my snow-white adult dogs. Obviously, Bambi had done his usual stunt of rolling upside down and sideways in the freshly mown, damp grass. He stood there, short poodle tail wagging like crazy, his clipped poodle coat green from head to toe. He was enjoying the fuss made over him, I suspect.

Father said, "Angel, that is an adult dog. We came to buy a puppy."

Her mother added, "Oh no, your Dad and I don't like green, dear. The nice lady is holding that cute puppy you liked. Take another look at the cute puppy."

The sweet little angel fell to her knees and gathered the green dog into her arms. She buried her little face in his green fur and declared, "You said I could pick the puppy and this is the one I pick. I want this green puppy." Bambi licked her cheek and wiggled his rump, loving the attention. He snuggled in her arms, pink tongue lolling.

"Uh, Angel, I don't think the lady wants to sell her adult dogs," Father said.

"Is he for sale?" Mother asked.

"No, no," I answered. "He is the father of the puppies you came to see, and of course he's not for sale."

"I want, I want, I want! You promised I could pick the puppy," Little Girl whined. She was now curled on the floor with green Bambi, her arms smothering him tight against herself. As for Bambi, he was starting to look a bit worried about being held down that way.

"Uh, how much would you take for the green dog?" Father asked.

"He's not for sale—ever," I replied.

"Look, if that is what our little sweetie wants, then that is what she gets," Mother argued.

"Ain't going to happen," I answered firmly.

"We could pay double," Father said.

"How much? Let's get this over with," Mother said.

To make a long story short, they didn't buy a puppy. Bambi stayed and soon was snow white again. That little critter daughter kicked and screamed a bit when they hauled her back to their car and strapped her in. Something about a green dog or nothing was the last thing I heard her yell when they pulled out of my yard.

* * *

I had been advertising an older, well-trained horse for sale for a child's mount. For the past few years, the senior gelding had been teaching little ones confidence until they could move on to a younger, faster horse. He adored children and, except for a bit of arthritis, was more than able to bring joy to some wee two-legged munchkin at his slow-going pace. He sold quickly after his ad had only been in the paper a couple of days and went to a good home with caring people.

So I was a bit surprised to see a truck pull into my yard that weekend, as I was not expecting company. A handsome young couple stepped out of the vehicle with their bouncing blonde boy of about three years old. I greeted them with a handshake and asked how I could help them. The gentleman explained that they were sorry they had not spoken to me before coming, but they had been visiting a friend of mine who told them about the child's horse I had for sale. They had just bought an acreage and needed to buy a very trustworthy horse for themselves and their child as they loved horses but had little experience with them. My friend had tried to call me, but since I was outside, I didn't pick up the phone. She then gave them directions to my place.

I explained that the gelding was sold already. I could see their little guy's eyes as big as saucers as he looked at the other horses munching grass near by. I offered to take them into the pasture so he could at least pet them. We stood amongst the quiet broodmares and their foals, the happy couple chatting up a storm with me about wanting to learn all about country living and the horses they hoped to own. The boy soon tired of petting horses and wandered away from them, busy as a bee picking up sticks to examine and talking to himself.

When he gave an excited squeal, we stopped talking to see what he was so enthused about. "Toad, Mommy. I found a toad," he happily cried out, his little hands cupping it with great care. Short legs churning away, he headed for their truck, careful not to drop his precious cargo.

His mom laughed, "He found his first toad in his grandmother's garden earlier this year. He insisted on bringing it home, and we had a terrible time getting him to release it on the edge of our lawn near some trees. Since then, he found another one at some friend's place and we had to keep it in a box for him until he went to sleep before we could release it too."

I thanked her for being so kind and for understanding

that toads should not be kept in captivity but returned to their natural habitat immediately, as they would not survive well in a captive environment. The father gave a slight shudder and promised me faithfully that the toad would not be in his son's possession long, as he did not like frogs and toads. I just smiled; the mother didn't mind them, but the man of the family sure seemed a bit squeamish. By then, we were back at their vehicle. The boy continued to keep his hands cupped gently over his new friend. His mom had to lift him into the truck and buckle him in as the boy talked up a storm to the toad, occasionally parting his fingers only enough to blow it a kiss.

We shook hands again, and I said I would keep my eyes open for quiet, well-trained older horses for them. It is always a pleasure to meet such nice people, and I had enjoyed their visit greatly. They waved as they backed their truck up and turned to leave my yard. I waved happily back.

They pulled out onto the road, but instead of picking up speed, they stopped. Truck trouble perhaps? I watched, and suddenly the driver's-side window was rolled down. I heard the little boy screaming, "My toad, my toad!" Then it happened—the father threw that poor, defenceless toad out the window onto the gravel road! He then sped away, the boy's screams drowned out by the roar of the motor and the rapidly rolled-up window.

I just stood there dumbfounded. So much for being a nice young family, and so much for turning the boy's toad loose as soon as possible in a safe way without upsetting their little pride and joy. I could feel my blood starting to boil. Boy, had I been duped! I like toads, darn it! I like all living creatures. I had memorized their home phone number in case I found a suitable horse for them. They would be getting a phone call from me all right, and it wouldn't be a pleasant one either. Spitting nails from my clenched jaws, I stormed out onto the road to see if the toad was damaged beyond help.

And there the poor toad lay. Slightly shattered and smelling pretty awful for a toad. Just laying there, dead. And I started to laugh. I laughed so hard that I was wrecking my bladder and had to cross my legs.

And the toad? Well, he was the roundest, plumpest, palm-sized horse turd I had ever seen.

CHAPTER

9

The Queen Lady

HER REPUTATION WAS WELL KNOWN. Truth be told, she really didn't know much about horses at all. But having married a man with money—a lot of money—she was hell-bent on spending it as fast as he could make it. With her long legs, dyed blonde hair and two-hour morning ritual of applying 40 tons of makeup, she was his prized wife, and he loved her with a passion. He never questioned how she was spending his money. Since he knew nothing about horses himself, he stayed out of the usual wheeling and dealing when buying and selling them. He built a huge barn for her and also an extravagant arena, working pens and holding pens—whatever she wanted.

She had answered an ad I was running for a very nice

two-year-old colt for sale. I was asking only what such a nice colt was worth; in fact, it probably wasn't enough for him. With an authoritative voice, she had informed me she was going to be in my neighbourhood the very next day and would stop and look at him. But she doubted she would pay that much. She never bothered to ask if the next day was convenient for me.

She was four hours late arriving and stepped out of her modern one-ton dually, attached to a horse trailer with living quarters worth more than my entire farm, without even a hint of an apology for being late. I approached her with my hand held out in greeting. She made no attempt to shake my hand, likely because her manicured long pink fingernails would have looked so out of place shaking hands with my scarred, calloused mitt. Self-consciously, I wiped my hand on my well-worn pants.

Now, I always lock my herd of dogs up when someone is coming, but after four hours, I'd figured she was a no-show and had turned them loose again. They greeted her with great enthusiasm, jumping all over her starched $150 blue jeans. A six-month-old pup stood on her hind legs and pawed upwards at the lady's gold-encrusted belt buckle. I almost lost it when she calmly nailed that pup with one of her $500 cowboy boots, knocking the pup back about six feet. Looking up, she saw my "you are about to die" facial expression and said, "I thought it was going to bite me."

After checking the 8-pound pup to make sure it was

okay, I locked it up in the house with the rest of my, on average, 14-pound vicious guard dogs, and I headed for the horse corrals.

I opened the door of my tack building and pulled out a halter with a lead rope attached. As I headed for the herd, she told me in a no-nonsense voice to catch the horse she was there to see. Hello, lady, I thought to myself, why am I carrying this halter?

The two-year-old lowered his head into the halter and nudged me with his nose to ask what I was up to. I moved him toward the main corral, and he followed quietly with no resistance. The lady fell in behind him, waving her arms and clicking to him with her tongue as if he didn't know how to lead. Good colt that he was, he ignored her. Once inside the pen, I turned the colt to fasten the gate, but the lady was already doing it. It was a simple chain fastener on a manufactured gate, but she did it wrong.

I hitched the lead rope around the snubbing post in front of my tack building, which I used for saddling horses. Then I stood back for the queen to examine the colt. She sniffed around him like a dog thinking about its next meal. She pushed on his hip, making him take a quick step to the side to regain his balance. "Well," she said, "I think he is lame. Did you see how he had to move because he is in pain?"

I scratched the back of my head under my ball cap, played with my cap for a second and said, "Yup, you're right, no use buying this horse. I'll turn him loose, and thanks for coming."

"No, let's see how he goes under saddle," she said. "He isn't a bad-looking colt. Just tack him up, and I'll decide if I want him."

Now folks, here is what my ad in the magazine had said: "Two-year-old gelding, top bloodlines, will make a barrel racer. Halter broke only, gentle and very willing." Hello, queen lady? I said to myself. Then out loud I said, "What ad in the magazine were you answering? This is a two-year-old colt, advertised as only halter broke. He is only rising two years old now; you must have your ads in the paper mixed up. I think you have made a mistake here."

Darn, did she get mad! I had just accused her of being less than perfect. I cannot even describe what she blathered about because I couldn't really understand any of it. Something about her time was precious, she was tired of horse sellers with excuses—I don't really know.

So I had one of my think-quick moments (they don't happen very often, trust me). I knew my colt was quiet and well handled, so I unhitched the halter from the snubbing post and swung up on him bareback as gentle as possible. He grunted a bit from my weight and, knowing he was no longer tied, moved out real nice with me on him. He pretty much went where he wanted to, with me only pretending to steer him around with the halter. Being so quiet, he put up with me on his back, although I could tell he would have preferred to be snoozing in the shade of the poplar trees right about then.

The queen stood there, tucking her expensive shirt into her starched jeans and adjusting her really expensive belt buckle, then said, "Good enough. I don't have all day. Put a saddle on him and I'll ride him."

Well, now I was on a power trip. That good two-year-old had put up with me, so I snubbed him up again. I opened the tack-shed door, got my old bronc saddle out and tacked that colt up, nice and easy. He just stood there and blew through his nostrils a couple of times to let me know that he was getting edgy about all this happening to him in one shot. I tightened that front cinch really, really slowly. I left the back cinch on my old bronc saddle kind of loose. I led the colt around a bit. I doubled up the lead shank to the halter, making a single rein. Then I stood back.

The queen was a mite clumsy swinging up. She turned that saddle on a first-time saddled colt just enough to pinch him real good. She then yanked on the left side of the lead shank to the halter and all hell broke loose. I must say this for the queen lady, she lasted a good two jumps before doing a face stand in the corral dirt. The colt then hit the gate and was gone, bucking his fool head off, leaving the queen lying there in the dirt. Now me being me, I was all so careful helping her up. She appeared to have no broken bones, but her makeup was wrecked with her moaning, groaning and rubbing dirt off her face. That colt came back to the corral at a dead run, blowing flame out of both nostrils. He skidded to a halt about two inches from her belt buckle. The look of horror on her face was priceless.

I walked her back to that monster truck of hers, and she never said a word as she climbed in. I didn't bother to point out that the side of her jeans was covered with fresh, grass-green horse manure. I figured she could discover that all on her own.

Darn it. It's been years now, and she hasn't been back. I suspect that she is never going to buy a horse from me. I am so heartbroken.

CHAPTER

10

Lessons from a Tramp

I WAS NOT IMPRESSED WHEN WONEAR, my small mixed-breed female, decided to mate with Old Jack, my Jack Russell, without my permission. Wonear and I had a long talk that evening about my responsibilities and her responsibilities. She never did it again after listening to my lengthy lecture.

The resulting pup that graces my home and land today looks a lot like Tramp from the old movie *Lady and the Tramp*, and she sports the name with pride. Tramp started teaching me lessons about dogs even before she was a full year old.

Two slim coyotes ambling across the neighbour's land in search of a fat gopher dinner stopped to watch the small dog streaking toward them, tongues lolling and grins on their furry faces. Wise enough to leave the country if a large farm dog set out after them, they showed no fear of the pint-sized hurricane rapidly approaching. In fact, the pair of them knew they could easily dispatch such a small dog in minutes should they choose to.

Tramp was going full out when she hit coyote number one in the shoulder, knocking his front end out from under him. I think the coyote was too surprised to react with his teeth. Twisting free from her grasp on his neck, he broke and ran. Coyote number two was next on her list. Tramp went at him a bit high, and her forward momentum carried her right up and over his back. The second her feet hit the ground on the other side of him, she was already spinning and going in lower this time. I couldn't see where her teeth connected, but he shook her off by leaping high in the air and then lit out after the other one.

My screeching and hollering to come back finally entered her hard-headed noggin, and she trotted proudly back, head high, tail carried like a flag. She passed me with her mouth full of gray coyote fur and her deep brown, amber-flecked eyes a'gleaming. I had just learned that a small, slightly insane dog can put the run on coyotes and live to tell about it.

I also learned that a small dog's thick rope of a tail can break old windows—in fact, two windows so far. Tramp does not like to be confined. When placed in the pen outside, she leaped onto the picnic table, then, as graceful as a cat, up onto the four-inch-wide windowsill. Balancing with front and back feet carefully placed in front of each other, she would look in at me and begin to wag her tail, whap, whap, whap against the glass. It didn't take long before the glass cracked in a ragged line. I removed the picnic table and repaired the window with bathtub caulking.

Seated at the computer with my back to the couch, I was not aware that Tramp was sprawled on the back of the couch against that particular window. Not until she began to wag that fool tail of hers. The second I told her to get down off the couch, she wound her tail up to full force. I removed Tramp from the living room and eventually repaired that cracked windowpane with the same good old bathtub caulking. This tail of hers reminds me of an upset rattlesnake—nothing serious until it gets wound up and strikes.

Eventually she taught me that my five-foot fences were a piece of cake for her to jump. Now she comes and goes as she pleases. She prefers hunting in the wee morning hours or at late dusk and doesn't quit until she has made at least one catch. Mice, gophers, ducks, foolish magpies, one weasel that drew blood on her before succumbing, and her greatest challenge: muskrats. Her lips, eyes and ears are covered with battle scars from those varmints. Tramp now weighs in at 19 pounds of solid-steel muscle. I weighed an old grandpappy muskrat she caught a while back. He weighed 18 pounds. It was her only catch that was just too heavy to hold in her jaws while jumping back into the yard. She guarded him all night until I could relieve her of her sentry duty the next morning.

Old Tramp stands on the four-inch-wide deck railing. From this favourite perch, she can easily watch for a potential rodent dinner out in the horse pasture. GAYLE BUNNEY

So why don't I take her to bed with me at night since she hasn't yet mastered opening the bedroom door to go on her hunting sprees? Well, think of her tail for a second. You have no idea how much fun it is to be whapped by that thing in the night.

I know that she is a danger to herself with her unquench-able thirst for teaching me lessons on what dogs can do if determined enough. But except for a porcupine-quill episode and getting skunked once too often, Tramp had survived serious injury—until last year, that is.

My whole pack of small-breed dogs had charged

through the dog door to see what Tramp had cornered that morning. From her deep bark, they knew it had to be something exciting. I also knew that bark. It indeed meant she was hunting and had her prey in sight. I figured another fox had made the mistake of having a nap under one of my old outbuildings. With the pack's help, he would soon be making tracks for parts unknown, Tramp hot on his trail but outrun once again by the fleet creature.

Well it wasn't a fox under the building; it was a cat on top of the building. The cat sat curled on the steep roof, its growls punctuated with hisses of contempt for the silly dogs below. There wasn't a dog in the world that could get him now. I knew that the cat was safe, and that the dogs could not harm him. Once they calmed down a bit, I would call them back into the house for the afternoon to give the feline time to make his escape. But someone had forgotten to tell Tramp that the cat was safe and secure on his perch. She circled the building, so intent on the cat that she simply mowed down the other dogs in her path with her chest, without apparently seeing them. Then it happened!

Beside the wall of the building was a jumbled pile of ancient boards waiting to go to their final resting place at the local dump. Tramp vaulted up onto the pile, balanced there for a second, and with those steel springs hidden in her powerful back legs she made the leap straight in the air. Her clawing front toenails caught the roof's wooden shingles, her shoulder muscles strained and she was on the roof.

That cat's hair rose straight on end. He stood frozen, he couldn't even spit or hiss. Dogs don't get on high roofs, hadn't anyone told this dog? Perhaps he believed he was just having a bad cat dream. That roof was not only high, it was a V-peaked roof with an incredibly steep angle.

Tramp now had four sets of scrabbling toenails under her, and she shot up that side of the roof going full out. She reached the peak, missed the cat and over she went. To me, it appeared she was going in slow motion as she tried to put the brakes on. She hit that oh-so-long-way-down ground with a thump that scared the other dogs so badly that they headed back to the house for safety. The cat remained in a rigid pose, more than likely in some kind of cat shock. Tramp raised herself slowly to a standing position. Her eyes were glazed and her breathing laboured.

The vet handed me the rather large bill and explained that although Tramp was not permanently injured, it would take lots of healing for her to get back to her old self again. He also muttered something about not giving him any more yarns about a little dog's injuries from falling off a roof all by herself.

Lesson learned—don't expect vets who have heard every story in the book to believe that a small-breed dog managed to scale the wall of a building chasing after a cat and then fell off the other side of a high, peaked roof. But then I suspect that few vets have ever met a real, true Tramp either.

CHAPTER

11

I Can't Resist a Good Bull

CATTLE HAVE ALWAYS BEEN A big part of my life, from my 4-H steers that I loved dearly to the pail-bunter calf that I broke to ride when she was a yearling. I'll never forget the stunning beauty of a newborn Jersey heifer calf with its big brown eyes and eiderdown-soft hair—far cuter than even a newborn whitetail fawn.

And Old Pete, my milk cow. Old Pete was so tame that she kept the grass mowed on the front lawn—and kept that lawn nicely fertilized too! I made the mistake of opening the house door and letting her into the kitchen to drink when the barn water was not working. She had waltzed through that doorway neat as a pin, then drank about 30 gallons from the kitchen sink, drinking it as fast as the open tap would give it. Unfortunately, she then didn't fit back through the open doorway to freedom outside. Her swollen water-filled belly got stuck tight as a drum in the doorway. I was a'hollering to get going, and she was a'trying. Then that "fertilizer" started coming. It was not a pretty sight. I had someone come to fix the barn water the very next day.

I have always had a special feeling for bulls. My dad raised registered horned Herefords, as my grandfather also had. Dad was fussy about what was a good bull and what wasn't, so when he kept a few back to raise and sell as two-year-olds to other breeders, you knew they were good bulls. Their pedigrees were the best; their conformation and disposition were the best.

Even as a young girl, I had a stubborn "my way or the highway" disposition. I suspect Dad only kept me because he had no choice in the matter, or perhaps because he wasn't allowed to run me through a fall heifer-calf sale listed as a crossbred, good-looking but of questionable disposition. I was about 11 years old when I got it into my head that if I couldn't have things my way, I would just run away from home. Of course, I decided to do it during a savage prairie blizzard. I bundled up and stormed out of the house into a sheer whiteout of blowing snow and howling wind. Being born on the prairies, I knew how to stay on course and not drift with the wind. If you let the wind push you in a white-out blizzard, you'll be out on the open prairie awful quick and then you're toast.

I Can't Resist a Good Bull

What do you mean the bull doesn't like me? Look how friendly he is!
MARGO MORTON

I knew where I was going first. I wanted to say good-bye to my pet bulls before heading out. They loved me and would never tell me to behave myself like my parents seemed to like doing. All the young bulls were lying down in their shed, quietly minding their own business when I staggered in, already covered in snow and with icicles hanging from my nose. I'd only been running away for a short spell and was already half frozen. That didn't matter. I was not ever going back to the house. Pretty soon, my parents would be sorry they didn't let me rule the roost. I was running away for all the right reasons.

My two favourite bulls, Champ and Ape, were lying side by side, Champ facing east and Ape facing west. I knelt down and hugged them tightly, telling each of them about how silly parents' rules were. I rubbed their foreheads, which bulls like as long as you don't do it too hard. If you do, they tend to give you a good hard wham, because they get in a fighting mood, thinking they are rubbing heads with another bull. I played with their horns, which were perfectly curved downwards from wearing steel horn weights when they were younger. I told them I loved them and, come hell or high water, they would never have to have a ring in their noses that would hurt them, just so they could be shown in some fancy-pants bull sale.

Boy, it was cold. Maybe instead of just coming down here to say goodbye to my pets, I should bed down with them. I gathered fresh straw and filled the space between Champ and Ape. Then I crawled over top of Ape and buried myself in the straw. Champ swung his mighty head over me and then so did Ape. Their heavy neck dewlaps covered me like a living blanket. Exhausted and now warm as toast, I fell into a peaceful sleep.

It was morning when I finally stirred. Sometime during the night, Ape had stood up, turned around and ever so gently had lain back down. His huge body still warmed me, his breath hot on my drowsy cheek. His left horn rested against my ribs. I was at peace.

Wait, my tummy was rumbling. I was running away and

had forgotten to pack groceries. This would not do! Nobody on God's green earth likes food more than I do. Champ belched and the fumes darn near did me in. Ape tried to lie flat on his side and darn near squished me. My left foot felt overly warm, and I saw it was covered with fresh fertilizer. Jeez, I had to go to the bathroom.

Well, I never ran away again, but if I had, I would have packed some food to go. The thing is, once I was back in the house, I was denied breakfast and sent to my bedroom. I could have starved to death!

As I drifted into keeping only horses and dogs, my keen interest in bulls became a memory. Until the drought year of 2002, that is. Now, I have the best neighbours in the world, especially the ones who own the quarter of land that my acreage nestles into. This is prime cropland, but the deadly drought of 2002 meant farmers and ranchers fenced a lot of it to run their cattle on. So when my neighbour Roger fenced and turned his cows loose, my dogs and young horses couldn't believe their eyes. A horse that had never seen a cow before tore out my own fenceline in fear of those hairy beasts that were out to eat him alive. My pack of wee dogs quickly got the run put on them.

I was happy, even if my animals were not. The two-year-old colt could not accept these strange beasts next to his personal space. No matter how many times I carefully explained to him that they were not bears or cougars, he continued to shake at the sight of a couple of

Charolais-cross cows coming up to the fenceline to say hello to him. I sold him as soon as possible so he could have some peace of mind.

Late fall and winter come rapidly to our northern Alberta country. Roger came to bring the cows and calves home, along with the two bulls he was running with the cows. The cows and their babies were easy to move, but those two mature bulls got all hot and cranky and refused to go home in an orderly fashion. Bingo! I had bulls back in my life. I was happy. When freeze-up arrived, Roger came back for his bulls as their only source of water would be frozen solid in the dugout. I was some miffed, let me tell you. Just because he owned them didn't mean he could come looking for them. I pointed out the full water tub and the pile of top-quality horse hay they preferred over their regular hay. Roger smiled, waved and headed off to do his other hundred waiting chores.

I was already watering and feeding those two suckers the best horse hay I owned—and wondering what in tarnation was wrong with my head. These were mature, older, herd sires, just good pasture bulls but not the friendly bulls I remembered from my youth. I named one Big Red and the other one Old Yeller, due to the colour of their hides. I set out to be their friend. Unlike my dad's bulls, they hadn't been spoiled and loved as youngsters, or groomed, fed an exact diet, or been halter broke with loving care. They were just bulls.

To start with, even with my electric fencer plugged in, when the dogs harassed Big Red and Old Yeller, they sometimes came ever so ever neatly through or over the fence in a bad frame of mind. The yowling pack of small beasts would retreat to my house and up the three small steps. The fence usually stopped Big Red, but Old Yeller hated those yappy little mutts so much, he once tested all three of the house steps while I prepared to pile furniture against the closed door for extra strength should he keep coming.

I figured what Big Red and Old Yeller really needed was love from humans for the short time they had here on earth—or at least for the short time they would have in my presence. Twice a day, I started giving them store-bought oats. It worked! Big Red got all cuddly, and I was falling in love. I only fed him the bucket of oats when I was protected by a solid timber corral fence, but I was able to scratch his head and neck, and he got to liking that. Old Yeller ate out of the bucket held safely between sturdy planks, instead of wire fencing, but when I reached through that fence to touch him, he splintered a couple of planks that one day. But he was coming along, I tell you.

When Roger came back again for those two bulls, I saw a tear in Big Red's eye, and I swear Old Yeller looked back at least twice at the good home he was leaving. At least I thought he was thinking about my home, but it was hard to tell with his bellowing, pawing the dirt and threatening to hook the side of Roger's pickup truck.

I miss Big Red and Old Yeller. Before I am done in, I'm going to get myself a good team of oxen. It's been a dream of mine since I was knee-high to a jackrabbit. A nice, big matched pair of oxen. I am going to raise them from calves, and they will be the best team ever—a team of steers, by the way, not bulls. Steers are much more friendly due to their little operation, if you get my meaning.

CHAPTER

12

Old Angus and Shady

I WAS BORN AND RAISED in the country, where you never say no to a friend in need. That just doesn't happen with us old-style country folk. But that doesn't mean that you sometimes don't regret it.

A dear friend of mine was in a peck of trouble. Brenda and her husband Rick were having a new home built. Once the new home was ready, their old house would be removed from their city lot and the new one placed on the existing foundation. It sounded simple enough. Well, it wasn't! Removing the old house and installing the new house meant tearing out the backyard fence that contained their two beloved dogs. The fence should only have been down for a couple of weeks, tops, but those weeks became months when everything that could go wrong did go wrong. They had no fence, no home and no place to keep their dogs.

Of course I will take your dogs! I agreed. Don't worry about a thing. I will come to the city and pick them up lickety-split. They will love it here on the farm. I know how much you love them, and I promise to love them too.

I stared at the size of Shady with bugged-out eyes. I hadn't realized that St. Bernards came that big. She ambled over to me like a Shetland pony with furry feet. Her whole body wiggled with joy at meeting me. She leaned against my legs, and I struggled to not tip over. Glancing to the left, I watched my next charge come into view. He was a splendid old fellow if ever I saw one. Old Angus had some age on him, but every inch of him was as a golden chow chow was meant to be. He wandered by me like a king who thought me beneath even a quick sniff from His Highness. This one will take some work, I thought to myself. But I was betting that in no time flat he would accept me as an equal and not as a mere lower-class country peasant.

Brenda was in tears. She had no choice but to give me her faithful friends. She loaded Shady and Angus into the back seat of my car, her voice quivering. I assured her I would bring them back to the city for visits and that she could trust me to care for them. She nodded, knowing I love animals. We headed off on the road home to the farm. My back seat generally holds a dozen of my small-breed goofballs. With these two, it was plumb full of hair, four eyeballs and Shady's humongous wagging tail thumping away on my rear side window. Whap, whap, whap went that tail. I hoped the glass would hold up to the assault.

It was a long trip to the city and back, so I pulled into a drive-through fast-food restaurant. At the takeout window I tried to make myself heard over the loud whapping sounds of Shady's tail. "Yes, I want to try one of those new Flame Thrower burgers you guys are advertising. And a black coffee. I think I'm going to need it before long. No, I have shut my car off, that whapping noise is not my car engine knocking. Hello? Can you hear me?"

Coffee and burger on the front seat, I headed out onto the highway for home. On a straight stretch with little traffic, I reached over and partially unwrapped the burger. That new Flame Thrower burger smelled wonderful. Eyes never leaving the road, I raised it to my waiting lips. I took a bite and chewed thoughtfully. I took a second bite and thought more about this new burger. It wasn't too bad, I guess, but why on earth did they put that slimy, blah sauce on the outside of the bun? It just wrecked the whole burger experience.

I think this is the appropriate time to explain to you just how much St. Bernards drool. Of course, Shady's head was hanging over the car seat as her whole body filled the back seat. That wasn't any new, wonderful sauce on this burger, it was doggie drool. I'm sorry, but I've never been able to stomach another Flame Thrower burger. I just don't have it in me.

Shady settled into farm life like she was born to it. My wee dogs were scared to death of her for weeks because when she tried to play with them she kept clumsily stepping on them. They had to learn to stay out of her way. And the horses spooked at first, perhaps thinking a brown and white bear had come to live there. I quickly learned to wipe drool off the table, the chairs, the floor and my body parts while it was still moist. I got into the habit of tucking a "drool rag" into my hip pocket when I dressed in the morning.

As for my precious old Angus, I never did become anything but a lowly peasant to this king. But we loved each other, and I came up with solutions to living with an elderly chow chow.

Shady didn't fit through the spaces between the wooden plank fencing into the horse corrals, so I had to open the gates. She would amble through with me as I cared for the horses. Angus did fit. Although up to three times the size of my wee pack of maniacs, he was nowhere near Shady's size. The trouble with King Angus was that he expected me to open gates for him too. The other problem with His Highness was that while Shady was beside me all the time, he was not. He took his time wherever he went and followed me only when he thought it was worth his while to do so. While out in the pastures or in a corral hard at work, my mind on the task at hand, I would hear "woof." A deep, demanding "woof." A right-now "woof." Turning, I would see Old Angus standing at a horse gate. Just standing there, staring at it. Not moving, just waiting for me to get my rear in gear to come open the gate for him.

When I failed to break into a run to answer his lordly summons instantly, he would give two or three deeper woofs with a bit of a snarl thrown in. If I was still not fast enough for him, he would grab the steel bars of the gate in his mighty jaws and tug at them. Unfortunately, if one of the wee dogs came near him when he was losing his patience with my poor service, he would turn and take it out on them. How did he do this? By raising one old hind leg and peeing on them. I soon learned to always run to open the gates for him. It was just so much easier than bathing some poor dog in the tub to remove Angus's mark.

Being a chow chow, and especially being a regal, elderly chow chow, Angus had no time for childish nonsense from the other dogs, the horses or me. He pretty much treated all of us the same way. We were beneath His Majesty. As time went on, he seemed to forget about such mundane things as horses and the world he lived in. He didn't wander around them, he wandered through them. On some mission that was only in his own mind, he went where he darned well felt like. Under horses' bellies, through deep water in sloughs, anywhere at his own elderly pace.

My gentle two-year-old gelding Raven was fascinated with Old Angus. He followed that dog everywhere in his pasture. Angus ignored him—just another peasant not worth his time. Raven was as gentle as a kitten with Angus.

More than once, he would be following Angus at the old dog's slower-than-molasses-in-January speed and reach down, and with great care not to catch the old dog's tender skin in his teeth, he would pick up old Angus by his thick fur and stand there with the dog's feet just a couple of inches above the ground. Angus just kept walking in mid-air. Gently, Raven would release his hold on the fur, and Angus would hit the ground still moving. Raven never paid much attention to the score of other dogs, just to his buddy Angus.

As time went on, Angus required daily pills to keep him healthy. I would place his pills in a cut-up piece of wiener, his all-time favourite treat. But the problem was that he removed one too many pieces of my fingers when I gave him the treat with the hidden pill. Some may say his eyesight wasn't that good anymore. I beg to differ. Old Angus simply believed me so much beneath him that my fingers and my blood just didn't matter. So I put my mind into high gear. He needed his pills three times daily. My hands needed to remain intact. He wouldn't take the loaded wiener treats out of his food dish or just dropped in front of him. I may have been his servant, I thought, but I have some smarts too, you old beggar!

Barbecue tongs. Yup, barbecue tongs. Three times daily, I put his pills into the little chunk of wiener and offered it to him clutched in the grip of my barbecue tongs meant for flipping steaks on the grill. I think Angus may have missed the bits of human skin for added flavour, but I felt a whole lot better about it.

Old Angus and Shady

A while back, some long-distance friends showed up out of the blue. I offered to barbecue steaks for supper. The husband let me know in no uncertain terms that he would do the barbecuing as no one was quite as good at cooking steaks as him. (I suspect his wife had told him that many times so she didn't have to cook supper.)

When he came looking for tongs to flip the steaks, he spied Old Angus's tongs hanging on the porch wall. I didn't bother to tell him why they were so twisted and mangled. I just smiled to myself. After all, Angus didn't drool. It couldn't be all that bad.

CHAPTER

13

Weed Whackers and Lawn Mowers

I HAVE BEEN KNOWN TO HAVE a bit of fun with people's minds sometimes. It breaks up the monotony of my daily chores. I remember one young teenager I hired for the summer who took me at my word no matter what I said.

I have a screen door separating my kitchen from my living room. I know it sounds strange, but it keeps dogs that are not well housetrained off my living-room carpet. No stepping over a barrier or a child's safety gate for me. Instead, I open the screen door when I go back and forth from the kitchen to the living room. The first day this young fellow worked for me, he surveyed the screen door and asked how come it was there. I never hesitated, "In the summertime, it lets the cool air from the living room pass through into the kitchen so it stays cool in the heat of the day too."

He nodded his head at the wisdom of what he had just heard, "I think Mom and Dad should have a door like that too at home because our kitchen gets really hot in the summer."

I had installed a second doggie door so the dogs in the living room could also go out to do their bathroom duties. They could zip through the doggie door into the small pen I had built for them at the front of the house. I had made one rather annoying mistake when building that pen. I had no way to get into it to mow the grass unless I pushed the lawn mower up onto the deck at the back of the house, through the kitchen and then through the living room.

About the third time the teenager showed up to help, he walked into the house and saw me coming out of the living room with the lawn mower. He had to ask, "Why did you have your lawn mower in the living room?"

I had to answer, "Surely your Mom has to mow the carpet in your living room at least once in a while too?"

Again he nodded his head over the wisdom of mowing one's carpets and replied, "Oh yes, of course she does, but Mom does it when I'm at school so I just never see her doing it." I nodded my head in agreement with his mom doing this while the kids were at school. It would keep them from being in the way, wouldn't it?

Most people stick to mowing lawns with lawn mowers,

but most people don't hate weeds in their horse pastures as much as I do. Using chemicals against these increasingly unsightly and large weed patches, inedible for horses, was out of the question. I had nowhere else to put the horses to prevent them from coming into direct contact with what is basically a poison, and I didn't want my pack of dogs near the stuff either.

Gary P., a dear friend of mine from the good old days, pointed out that continual mowing of such weed patches, so that they were never allowed to go to seed, would eventually not only stop them from spreading but get rid of them altogether. Dear Gary failed to mention that this would be an ongoing battle for several years.

They don't make lawn mowers like they used to. I started mowing in my horse pastures with an already beat-up, second-hand green machine that I had purchased years before. I named that old mower "Freddie" after a tough kid from high school who also looked like he'd been in one too many fights out behind the barn. Freddie attacked those weeds year after year. On rough, rock-covered ground, he tied into weeds that were often close to three feet tall with intent to maim every one of them. He chewed his way through acres of them, smoke pouring out of his carburetor, his blades bent from rocks grinding against his rusted sides. He would cough and choke a bit when the going got particularly rough, but he never quit.

I picked up all the parts that were falling off him and

cheered him on the best I could. By year three, approximately four acres of weeds had been reduced to maybe an acre. Freddie and I were winning the battle. Occasionally I gave him a day of rest by just mowing the rock-free, level surface of my six-inch-high lawn grass around the house. He appeared bored with such an easy task and hardly smoked at all.

It was year four, and the month of June was coming up. I studied the small patches of weeds poking their horrid little heads up and grinned in anticipation of what was likely to be the last year-long battle between them and Freddie. As I was lovingly adding some much-needed oil to Freddie after his long winter rest, a never-had-to-mow-grass-in-her-life lady, who I sometimes found a bit annoying, pulled into my yard. "What you doing?" she asked in her perky voice.

"Feeding Freddie," I replied.

"Why don't you get a new mower?" she asked, peering down at his rusted frame.

"Because you don't have to be pretty to get the job done," I quipped while trying to work around her cutesy little body hovering over top of Freddie.

She said, "I heard one of your neighbours thinks you're totally nuts, you know." She flipped her hair and smirked a bit at telling me this grand news.

I screwed Freddie's oil cap back on and straightened up. "Nuts to my neighbour!" I snarled.

She didn't get my meaning and danced a little jig while

sweetly saying, "Yes, nuts. She thinks you're nuts for mowing your horse pasture all the time in silly patches first here and then there. She says she drives by and always sees you out there making your pasture look funny with leaving these big bald patches all over it. She says all the while your lawn is in desperate need of being mowed with the grass way too high." She bounced up and down in her perky high-heeled sandals, waiting to hear what I had to say in return.

Instead I fired up Freddie. One pull and he roared to life. The little lady actually gave a tiny scream, as Freddie was prone to sounding like an incoming jet when first fired up after his winter rest. He belched black smoke and shook so hard he was coming off the ground. One look at the lady's horrified face and I knew I had her right where I wanted her. Above the roar, I hollered at her, "Get back, get back, I think he's going to blow!" She let out a full-blown scream and fled to her car. Freddie coughed a bit and then settled back down. I just smiled.

Freddie passed away shortly after that episode. I think his heart just gave out when his handlebar rusted off and I couldn't bolt it back on. I purchased a new lawn mower, but it was never the same. The new one couldn't take the rocky ground or the three-foot-tall weeds. It spent most of its time in town being repaired, so my lawn sometimes reached a foot tall between mowings. I hope the neighbour lady noticed that my lawn really did need mowing that year.

I hope she also noticed that I wasn't out in the horse pasture mowing bald patches here or there either.

After Freddie died, I dug out the heavy-duty weed whacker my dad had bought me years ago. No spindly, twirling plastic strings on this baby. No sir! Three steel blades, four speeds and a harness to wear just to pack the weight of it. This puppy was the real McCoy! I named my whacker "Peter."

And weeds be damned. Those annoying poplar saplings that were growing up along my electric fencelines could make the fences lose power. It was time to attack them—and attack them right when a certain neighbour lady was driving by, so she could get a full view of me doing so.

I read the instructions carefully. I settled on the highest speed rating, number four. The instructions said that on high speed you could cut not only weeds but also small brush. I headed for the horse pasture. Some of those poplar saplings were now over four inches in diameter. Okay, maybe some of them had gone from brush-size to six- or eight-foot-tall trees.

Peter chewed through the overgrown saskatoon bushes just fine. He whined a bit about the smaller saplings but did his job. He started to smoke a bit on the four-foot-tall ones, making me almost break into tears remembering my old Freddie and his habit of smoking on the job. I hear that smoking is not good for you, but if Freddie could do it, so could Peter. Then I discovered that to cut those big eight-foot-tall ones, you could raise Peter away up over your shoulder like a baseball bat with the throttle open wide, line up that incoming ball (I mean, tree) and swing at it for a home run.

Peter chopped through those trees with little more than a low whine. It was awesome! I tried to make sure I cut down those bigger trees when a certain neighbour lady's vehicle was passing. She would slow down and gawk like a chicken at my property. Just plain nosy, I would say. Seeing Peter in action a couple of times sure stopped that gawking in a hurry. She didn't slow down much any more and didn't try to see what I was up to.

I heard last winter that maybe I wasn't a safe person to be around when out in the horse pasture. Thanks, Freddie. And you too, Peter!

CHAPTER

14

Magpie Splats

I WAS ON MY WAY TO TOWN to a very important meeting—
one of those do-or-die missions I'm famous for. Meetings
such as this one with my banker always got me revved
up like a 68 Ford on a straight stretch of highway. I was
showered and dressed in my newest blue jeans and even
wearing my "Sunday-go-to-meeting" shoes. With that shot
of perfume behind one ear, I was smelling kind of pretty for
a change too.

I know practically all the wildlife on and around my
property and recognized the daddy magpie that dive-
bombed my car before I got out of my driveway. This
particular old boy spent most of his time harassing the dogs
over their food, even though Tramp's snapping jaws had got

most of his tail feathers the year before. It hadn't stopped the bird from flying, but he sure couldn't corner in mid-air very well without his steering gear. He would head for tree number one and end up landing in tree number two with the most disgruntled look on his face.

That day, he glared through the windshield of my car the second I hit the brakes, so I had a real close look at him as he was screaming at me. Seconds later I spotted his petite mate sitting on a low poplar branch about three feet off the ground. Her cries of distress told me I had better investigate. I stepped out of the car and was instantly buzzed by daddy bird. I ignored him. Both a great horned owl and a hawk had removed part of my hair or hide in the past, and I had a lot more respect for them than for this silly magpie. There on the ground below Momma Bird was one of this year's babies caught up in the tall grass under the poplar. He was pretty tired, and his newly emerging feathers were bedraggled.

I knew this pair of birds but didn't know where their nest was. I picked up the baby and went looking for a nest down the ditch and fenceline. I stopped under numerous nests, old and new, but Mom and Dad continued their screeching and flapping without indicating I was at the right one. Back where I found him, I put the baby magpie down again. I ran for the house, grabbed an empty ice-cream pail, stuffed it with straw and wired it as high up in that tree as I could reach. Then I picked up the baby and put him in his

100

new nest. I flapped my own wings up and down to dry the perspiration so it didn't override my careful squirt of perfume, jumped in the car and roared off to town, knowing I was already going to be late.

It was a couple of hours before I pulled into my driveway again. The clearly visible, temporary nest was empty. Ma and Pa Magpie were several hundred feet down the fenced road allowance, both sitting on low tree branches and literally wailing in anguish. Sure enough, there back on the ground was their baby. After a couple of hours of fighting his way through tall grass and ground bush, he was close to being toast. He lay weakly on his side, mouth gaping from exhaustion, eyes closed. I had just acquired another rescued creature. Ma and Pa buzzed me steadily as I carried him to the house, cursing me as only magpies can do. Obviously they didn't realize I was trying to help.

I cut down a small poplar tree and set it up in my bedroom, rigging a temporary nest in it until the baby bird had the strength to hold on to a branch. He soon talked to me non-stop, from the time the sun came up until it went down in the evening. I fed him constantly, just like his parents would have done. His diet consisted of icky live earthworms with some dirt still attached, crushed puppy chow, a bit of hard-boiled egg and highly nutritious tubifex worms, used for fish food, but excellent for magpies as well. Thank heavens he didn't require feeding at night, as between feeding him all day long and catching some much-needed shut-eye,

The rescued baby magpie stayed in his tree when he wasn't being fed. "When is she going to feed me again? It's been an hour. I hope she brings another yummy, wiggly earthworm soon." GAYLE BUNNEY

I was always late getting the other animals cared for. While he was starting to gain his health back and looking pretty perky, I was starting to look like a bedraggled orphan.

The fun part was that he would wake up before me early each morning and fly from his tree to my bed. He would hop up and begin nibbling inside my ears or tugging on my eyelashes until I got up and fed him. He talked in a soft, sweet voice as he nibbled away, even checking out my nostrils on the odd occasion, but once he knew I was awake he would scream at the top of his voice that he was hungry.

His house-training went without a hitch. He preferred

to be fed on the bed or dresser, so I'd place a folded piece of paper towel under his back end before beginning to feed the front end. With the first bite, he would wiggle his butt and splat onto the paper towel right on schedule. He stayed in his tree when I wasn't catering to his demand for food. He was a very clean and intelligent bird and never once pooped anywhere in my bedroom except while in his tree, when it landed on the newspaper underneath for easy cleanup.

Once he was strong enough, I took him to the Wildlife Rehabilitation Society of Edmonton. There, along with some other rescued magpies, he was taught to be a wild magpie again. When they were adults, they were released together back into the wild.

I swear that he returned to my farm after his release, even though it would have been a long, unknown flight path. For a few weeks, a rather slim young magpie showed up and hung out with two fat old crows in a tree on my lawn. For some reason the crows tolerated him without driving him away, which they normally would have done. This young bird always talked up a storm when he saw me come outside. If I approached the tree, he would peer down at me with his head cocked, give a soft chatter and then, with one fast rear-end wiggle, he left his mark. A perfect splat!

CHAPTER

15

Snow Dump

"BE CAREFUL WHAT YOU WISH FOR" is an old saying with much truth to it. One winter a few years ago, most of us landowners were hoping for a good dump of the white stuff to make up for a couple of dry years so the horse pastures would be lush and green come spring. I think I prayed too much and too long.

By the middle of December, I was pretty much snowed in. My new red car was sitting there in all its glory in my garage because of the deep snow directly outside the garage door. I was taking my beat-up old four-by-four to town regardless of the additional cost of gas to drive it. With the hubs locked in low, at least I was chugging my way out of the yard. Did you know that there is a lot more room in a car's front seat, back seat and trunk for perishable groceries than in a single cab on a truck?

After another dump of snow, a truck and trailer from a horse buyer chewed up the deep snow in my yard by getting stuck a few times trying to jack the trailer around to the loading gate. This guy was a true gentleman, and I'll always hold him in the highest regard. Maybe I'm just getting old and jaded, but I kept waiting for him to come boiling out of the cab of his truck, snarling and spitting over the deep snow, kicking his tires and ranting with those unspeakable words some menfolk are prone to using when stuck after a long drive to get a horse and facing a long drive home. No sir—the gentleman did get out of his truck a couple of times but with an award-winning smile on his face. He was so pleasant about his truck and trailer tires being mired down in two feet of snow that I wanted to grab a shovel and help out. I wanted to, but mind you, I'm not really up to it at my age, and I hate shovelling big time.

A warm chinook wind came up that night and glazed those ridges of churned-up snow so they looked like sparkling diamonds in the moonlight. Of course, it turned bitterly cold again about the time I needed to get the four-by-four and skid some more round bales to the horses with a chain around them that was attached to the hitch on the truck. I mostly wanted to skid those 1,200-pound bales from west to east, but those deep, frozen ruts ran mostly from north to south. It just wasn't going to happen.

Thank heavens for friends. Garth showed up with his handy-dandy oversized Bobcat. That kitten of his was just a'purring, and he was soon finished down to bare earth in my yard and out into the horse pasture and corrals. If I'd wanted to, I am sure I could have skidded those bales with that cute little red car that was no longer trapped in the garage—that is, if the weather just would have cooperated for a while.

Then came another dump of snow, and another the next day with a bitter wind that blew drifting snow from the neighbour's land across my yard. The car was trapped in the garage again, and the truck was wise enough to think twice about even starting, let alone skidding bales. Well, I would feed the horses their hay with a pitchfork for now.

But let's get back to this problem about shovelling at my advancing age. First I had to shovel from the door of the house across the deck so the dogs could get out of the house. Then I took a rest and breathed deeply of the pristine, clear winter air. Next I slogged out to the horse corrals and shovelled out the hard banks of snow to open the gates. After another rest and more breaths of the wonderful winter air, I fed the horses. I took off my silly toque so the top of my head could get some fresh air.

When I slogged back to the house again, I noticed that all the dogs were running happily together. This was not a good thing! Cujo is kept separate so he and Mr. Higgins don't fight. Two male dogs can be like two guys after the same girl in a bar late on a Saturday night. Those guys in the bar need a couple of drinks to give them courage, but no consumable spirits were needed by two male dogs. I broke up the developing skirmish and put Mr. Higgins in the living room to sulk. He thought he could win a fight with Cujo, but I knew better. Yup, a large bank of snow went clear over top of Cujo's fence. The fence was five feet high; the bank of snow was six feet. Have I mentioned my age and how I feel about shovelling excessive amounts of snow?

Two hours later, the bank of snow was a 16-foot-high pile away from the fenceline. I felt like it was summer because sweat was dripping off me and my clothing was down to the bare necessities. I went into the house, intending to collapse in a stupor. Coffee—I needed an entire pot of coffee. But maybe not. The beautiful building I had put up for the dogs so they didn't all have to be in the house at the same time was blocked by a bank of snow that completely hid the carefully installed doggie door. It was a building heated to the same temperature as the house, a building where I had lovingly placed old furniture so that any dog using it felt like they were right at home. Heating it alone cost me a fortune. It was time to grab hidden reserves of strength from my English, Irish and Scottish ancestors. I could do this—just watch me. I come from a strong, hardy lineage.

My pack of midget dogs can travel on top of the hard drifts of snow. I cannot. I plowed though the snow like a bulldozer in slow motion, breathing heavy and feeling faint.

The dogs were there to support me. I was in waist-deep snow, but they were on top of the snow, which allowed them to lick the sweat dripping off my chin simply by standing on their hind legs. There were dog tongues everywhere.

With thoughts of retirement and living in a warm and sunny land, I leaned against the corner of the doghouse. I wanted to take off more clothing as I was too warm from the physical exertion, but I was afraid to. I'm just not good-looking enough anymore to strip down in plain sight of the road!

I caught my breath, my shovel just about ready to attack this final, hard-packed snowdrift. Then I saw them—faint tracks coming from the treed area of my pasture, through the dog fence and leading to a hole dug down and through the buried dog door of the building. Weasel tracks.

In the doghouse, I had food and water on the floor surrounded by furniture for the dogs. Mr. Weasel was a happy camper. He didn't have to hunt for food; he just moved in when the dogs couldn't. Smart weasel. I commended him and began shovelling. My pack helped by jumping up onto my back and shoulders as I was mired so deeply in the snow. I was too tired to curse or swear. Soon, as my shovel kept digging away at the door, I heard one frightened or perhaps mad weasel ricocheting off the walls. Too bad, little guy, I thought. I was on a mission and wasn't going to stop.

Exhausted, I finished and turned the door handle. I used the last of my strength to open the door. I stepped inside, mission accomplished. Wearing his wintertime coat of silky white, Mr. Weasel was not hard to spot. He stood up on the back of a big chair, fur fluffed out, teeth showing. Motionless, he glared at me. I raised my hand in greeting, not an easy task because my arms felt like they'd fallen off with the shovelling.

Mr. Weasel turned his lip up at me and headed for the open door. I panicked—my Great Hunters were all out there. Don't do it, Mr. Weasel, don't do it! He did not run through their legs. He moseyed through them, stopping occasionally to stand up and sniff a dog's belly. Not a single Great Hunter even saw him. Then he was gone, back to the wild.

I went back to the house figuring I'd stay inside until spring. Maybe by then my aching body would be healed up.

CHAPTER

16

Internet Dating
Cowgirl Style

WELL, IT HAS FINALLY HAPPENED. Advanced age and men-on-pause have rendered me a forgotten woman—forgotten and all alone in this big world of blue-jeaned, cowboy-booted, fast-talking, good-looking, horse-loving members of the opposite sex. The days of having one of those country boys around to help with chores seem to have come to an end. No matter what type of weather—rain, snow or wind—I am forced to do the chores all by my lonesome. I was not looking for help in the kitchen or laundry room, just some help with the outside chores. Not that I fully trust anyone else to do those chores, you understand, but it's still a lonely existence.

I scanned the online dating services a time or two and

got a good laugh out of them. The trouble was I needed a country boy of mature age to help around the farm. Maybe some hanky-panky once in a while would be good too, providing I wasn't too tired from those darn chores building up outside.

And then I saw it: a computer dating service for country people. I took a quick look at the available male members. There was nothing too fancy being advertised, but one or two looked promising, especially if you could gently re-educate them to understand just why they were single in the first place and what they would have to do to fit into your life. Maybe put some training on them to get them listening to commands a bit better. As it was free, I decided to write them a little email about needing some help on the farm. I used my best language and tried to be polite about asking how much they were worth. I didn't want to be stuck with a man critter just out for my money. Not that I have any, of course, but they sure didn't need to know that.

I didn't get a reply from either of them, but in my email inbox was a cute little message from the dating website telling me that I had to join first. Joining was free; all I had to do was fill out the membership form and soon I would have some help here on the farm. I got right down to filling out that form.

I was raised to be honest, and I answered all those questions with that in mind and pretty much told the truth. I smoke, swear and am known to be downright nasty until about noon every day. It's best not to touch me with anything shorter than a 10-foot pole before then. And I'm a tad overweight. In the part where you fill out what you want in a new mate, I was just plain honest: "Looking for a hardworking, no messing-around type of man. Best have money as I ain't got much; best be tough as some of my horses and dogs will take a chunk out of you if you're not tough enough to handle them."

Nothing! I scrambled to get my chores done every day so I had time to go check if anyone had written to me. Nothing! My feelings were getting a bit hurt because any man would be darn lucky to be associated with me. It had been a couple of long, lonely weeks. Finally, I got a message from someone. I was so excited I had to use the bathroom twice before opening up that email sent to me personally. I had snared myself a down-home boy sure as grass don't grow under fresh cow patties.

Nope. I couldn't receive the message until I paid to join. The free stuff was just to suck you in. I had to join—meaning pay money—to receive that message! I spent a good 24 seconds deciding if I was going to give my credit card number out over the Internet, then I went for it like an old mare in heat. The second I joined, I found out the message was from the darn website themselves, not a potential helper here on the farm. Now I was mad. I had joined just so some snotty Internet gal could tell me that my "personal resume" needed some tweaking in order for me to

112

get that new man into my life. All I had to do was follow instructions and they would teach me how to fill out my statistics on an Internet dating service so I would get more replies. They told me what to say and how to say it. I was pretty much broken by then. In fact, I was sobbing outright. So I hunkered down to redo my resume.

Now you folks into Internet dating listen close to what I'm going to tell you. It ain't pretty. The first rule is "Do not be honest." Lie through your teeth. Never admit you have bad habits. Never admit that you're anything but a loving, caring, kind-hearted, sexy person who has lots of money. When filling out the sections on what pleases you, say moonlight walks, dancing, cuddling in front of the fireplace and cooking fancy meals. Say you are perfectly proportioned; say any darn thing except the truth.

I am still single and loving it. Just me, the horses and the dogs. I never have to tell any of my four-legged companions to put the toilet seat down after going to the bathroom. Loving it.

17

The Leader of the Pack

IT WAS EARLY MARCH AND a good day to be alive. The day dawned bright and as warm as freshly buttered toast. With house chores completed, horses fed and yard cleanup done, I stood there in the sunshine and said to myself, "What a perfect day to take the dogs for a long walk." Whistling a happy tune, off I headed.

The dogs leaped excitedly around me, plowing through the deep, fresh snow and racing ahead, puffs of snow shooting in the air with each jump they made. The snow was deeper than my pack of small dogs were tall. One second they were visible, the next they disappeared. I switched from whistling to humming a tune because I seemed to be a bit short of breath. The snow was halfway to my knees, and

I was finding the going a bit harder than anticipated. "Good for the old heart," I told myself.

As usual, I walked in a circle across the land, and before long I decided to shorten the size of the circle a bit. That was when I hit the treeline and found myself in snow halfway to my waist. Huffing and puffing, I couldn't have hummed a tune now if I tried. This was turning out to be hard work. Soldier on, girl, soldier on! "Good for keeping my weight under control," I told myself.

Stopping to rest yet again, I leaned against a spruce tree and gazed at the splendour of the winter landscape. There wasn't a dog in sight. Turning around, I had to laugh because obviously I had been breaking trail for the pack for some time. My trail through the deep snow was filled neatly with one dog after another. I counted 22 dogs waiting in a perfect line for me to continue. With a deep breath, I pushed onward. As leader of the pack, it was my job to get us safely home. Sweat was soaking my Canadian Pilsner toque, and its warmth was annoying me, so off it came. I unzipped my Arctic parka and plowed on.

Glancing ahead, I was pleased to see that home was only another quarter of a mile away. I would stop for just one more wee break. The dogs must need it, I said to myself. Poor things! It had nothing to do with me being a bit exhausted. A dog in the line behind me barked in annoyance at yet another rest stop that was spoiling its fun, but the dog directly on my heels really got the message across

A long trail of happy dogs followed me in the deep, soft snow. GAYLE BUNNEY

when it promptly stood up on its hind legs and nipped me politely on my chubby rear end to get me moving again. I would have turned around and "politely" said something rude to the dog if I'd had enough strength left to turn my body. I plowed on, thinking that I'd drag out the weigh scale when I got home and check how much weight this exercise had helped me lose. I was betting that those tight jeans that I couldn't zip up yesterday would now fit perfectly!

116

We hit the plowed yard in single file, me weaving in exhaustion and the dogs tearing off in all directions, happy as larks. I didn't have the strength to get the weigh scale down off the top shelf, and it would have been too much work to see if the jeans now fit. But I was betting I'd lost megapounds. "Yup, good for the heart and good for the waistline," I reminded myself.

CHAPTER

18

Wildlife Tales

LIVING IN THE COUNTRY AS I DO, I have plenty of contact with the local wildlife. While I love all creatures, sometimes that can lead to some scary situations.

I live alone in an old house with many dogs but no other humans. The house is so old it has a dirt basement, which I call "the dungeon." I hate the dungeon and have to force myself to go down there to change the furnace and pump filters; otherwise I never, ever go down there. It is dimly lit by one lonely light bulb and full of menacing shadows.

One morning, I got out of bed and thumped my feet on the floor. Instantly there came three answering taps from the dungeon. I froze. Slowly I lifted my foot up and thumped it down again. Again I heard those three answering taps.

My hair stood up on my neck. I bravely came out of the bedroom and gazed at the closed basement door. Slowly, I opened the door and whispered, "Who are you. What do you want?" Lord thumping jackrabbits, it answered, "Tap, tap, tap!" A tiny scream escaped my throat, and I slammed the door shut and latched it tight again.

I sipped my morning coffee at the kitchen table, never taking my eyes off that door. I was frazzled big time, but horses, dogs and puppies had to be taken care of, and I began my daily chores. I pushed all thoughts of what certainly must be a ghost to the back of my mind.

Later in the day, I was busy doing what I do best: scooping poop. Lord have mercy, as I walked past the narrow basement window, the ghost began furiously tapping on the glass. With only the pooper scooper to defend myself, I faced the window, trying to see the ghost, the scooper raised to strike should it come through the casement. Nothing. I couldn't see a thing. I screamed at the ghost, "What in tarnation do you want?" It answered, "Tap, tappity-tap."

That did it. I was so scared I threw the scooper at the window and took off running. I didn't know where I was running to, but I was not going back in that house. Huddled out behind the garage, I began to give myself the pep talk of the century. It went like this: "Come on, you sissy. Come on, you wimp. What ghost on this planet stands a chance against you, the toughest, greatest, wildest, bronc-stomping fool woman of all time? Just grab some courage, you wimp!"

I stormed back into the house, grabbed a heavy flashlight (the biggest one I own so I could hit the ghost with it), threw open the basement door, took a deep breath and plunged down the rickety steps into the dungeon. I was ready to fight. That ghost was going to be some sorry for messing with my mind.

A poor frightened bird, a starling, which must have come down the chimney into the basement, pathetically went tap, tap, tap on the small basement window. His feathers were disheveled and his eyes sad from hours of being trapped in the dungeon. Once I got the poor starling up out of the basement and free, he flew away until he disappeared into the blue sky in the distance.

Now you know how much I believe in ghosts!

* * *

After the ghost episode, it had been a slow couple of weeks with not much excitement in my life. I was starting to feel a tad old; nothing was happening to get my pulse revved up, and I was starting to forget just what an adrenaline rush felt like. Heaven forbid that I don't get my weekly adrenaline rush!

The weather was just right for tackling the never-ending lawn mowing The horses could snooze in the shade, as they were doing a fairly good job of keeping the grass mowed in the pasture, but the dogs never did seem interested in mowing the grass on this side of the fence. Digging holes in the lawn is more their style. I hoped I wouldn't break an ankle stepping in one of their excavations while mowing.

I was still gassing up the mower when the dogs set up an awful ruckus under a tree at the end of my driveway. Obviously some little squirrel was sitting up in that tree laughing his head off at the silly dogs and probably flipping his daintily curled tail at them just to drive them even farther around the bend. Leaving the mower, I went halfway up the driveway and bellowed at the pack to get home, as they are not allowed near the road. For once, they all listened to me and ran back to sit crowded together on the steps. They sat there pretty quietly too, for dogs who think that quiet only happens for a couple of brief hours at night. Maybe all my hollering at them was finally paying off after umpteen years of sounding like a bull moose in the fall rut to get them to listen.

Turning my back on them, I once again got ready to power up my grass-eating machine. Within seconds, the squirrel must have made a dash from the driveway trees to the big spruce 30 feet from my doorstep because the pack tore off the steps toward the tree in howling agitation. I didn't see the squirrel but smiled while thinking how brave the little beggar was to make that mad dash even closer to the fool dogs and with me only scant feet away.

The mower roared to life, and I started on the closest section of lawn. I went around that part of the lawn, ended up at the big spruce tree, ducked under the branches and went around again. The dogs were all leaping at the squirrel in the tree, barking like fools and moving away for only a second to let me get by them. About the fourth time ducking under the branches, I realized I had to tighten the bolt on the mower blade. I stopped under the tree in the shade, relaxed for a minute and then looked up to see if I could spot the sneaky squirrel.

It's not every day you look up into a tree 30 feet from your doorstep and into the unfriendly eyes of a good-sized black bear! Up close like that, his claws looked like six-inch deadly daggers. I made it to the safety of the house in about two giant steps. I easily got the dogs locked up because instead of hollering at them, my voice was coming out all high-pitched and squeaky, which they were not altogether used to. With the dogs no longer able to harass him, Mr. Black Bear dropped down from my tree and loped away while grumbling to himself.

I'm telling you, I'm going to have a heart attack one of these days with these super-powered adrenaline rushes that keep happening to me.

* * *

It was the end of July, and we country folk were praying for rain. There had been lots of roaring thunder and lightning ripping across the sky in my area but no real rain to speak of. Finally, the thunder and lightning gave way to a downpour of beautiful rain. It was hitting the hard-packed, dry ground in the horse corrals and splashing up knee-high. Of course I was out in the corrals when the downpour started. Had I known that the afternoon shower was coming, I wouldn't have bothered to have one in the morning. I was soaked long before I could reach the house.

Once inside, I reached up to remove my dripping glasses, stopped and peered out through the windowpane in the door. In a patch of tall weeds in the horse pasture (which proves that weeds don't need rain to grow) I caught a glimpse of one of my little black and white dogs. It looked like it was Buttons out in the rain. She had brought home a leg from a winter-killed whitetail deer earlier that day, carrying it proudly over half a mile. I opened the door and whistled for her. I have distinct whistles for what I want my dogs to do, but Buttons ignored me. Intent on chewing away on the old deer leg, she never even raised her head out of that measly patch of weeds.

I was wet anyway, and I could hardly see through my dripping eyeglasses. If Buttons would not come to my whistle, I would just get wetter and go bring her in. I dived back out into the rain and strode towards Buttons while giving my come-to-me whistle the best I could through wet lips. My whistle was coming out more like a sputter; I had never realized before that your lips should be dry for really top-of-the-line whistling.

I pushed the tall weeds aside and reached for Buttons—but not for long! The skunk glared up at me through his beady little eyes and calmly turned his rump toward me. Now skunks and I go back many, many years. I will make a pet out of any wild creature, but skunks and I do not get along. I backed away slowly while Mr. Beady Eyes flicked his tail but thankfully did not let loose with what I can only describe as the worst perfume known to mankind. Once out of the immediate range of Mr. Skunk's perfume, I trudged toward the house, moving slowly because my eyeglasses were not just dripping rain but totally outdated, and I couldn't really see a thing.

Mr. Stinky Pants fell in behind me, following me at his own leisurely pace. I didn't bother to run. His head was facing me, not his tail, so he wasn't going to envelop me with the smell from hell. Besides, after almost having a ghost in my basement and a bear in my tree, a measly skunk simply could not give me much of an adrenaline rush.

As for Buttons, she was under the kitchen table with her deer leg all along. Like I said, time for new glasses.

CHAPTER

19

The Buffalo Runner

I HAVE A HEALTHY RESPECT for buffalo. About 15 or so years ago, getting chased by a less-than-friendly bull buffalo taught me that you really cannot outrun them on foot. Big, big, healthy respect. Now that I am older, my respect for them has grown even more.

One June day last year, I headed out on my daily walk with the pack of wee dogs, looking forward to a bit of exercise and enjoying the array of colourful birds, wildflowers and the occasional glimpse of non-threatening wildlife. You know—mice, gophers, a coyote loping away in the distance. I have the privilege of walking on my neighbour Roger's land, to the south. As I finished crossing his first field of clover, I perked up and watched for his cattle on the next quarter section. Those old cows protecting their calves and the bulls busy romancing those four-legged beauties do not take kindly to a pack of small, crazy-coloured coyotes disturbing their siestas or their daily lunch buffet. It's safer for the dogs and me to avoid those fertilizer-producing critters if at all possible.

Seeing no cows, I crawled through the barbed-wire fence and kept going. Then I scanned ahead, off to the right where the buffalo lived. The buffalo were nowhere near the fence-line; they appeared to be sleeping peacefully clear across their pasture. Good! If you think cranky cows protecting their calves and those super-sized, sex-happy bulls will put the run on my pack, they don't hold a candle to a buffalo's attitude of "Let's kill those 14-pound yappers." I am quite sure that the thunder of hooves as the herd descends on my pack of furry kids can be heard for miles.

I was busy enjoying life as I kept heading south, thinking that I should be able to walk a full three miles at that rate. Heck, maybe I would lose a quarter of a pound from all that exercise. Life was good!

Knowing that there were no gophers left for easy getting on Roger's land, half a dozen of my best gopher hunters headed into the buffalo pasture. Squeezing through the narrow squares of six-foot-tall, heavy-gauge wire fence, they swarmed the pasture. I wasn't worried as the buffalo herd was bedded down, chewing their cud while sleeping calmly in the hot sun.

There is one small and lonely building in the buffalo pasture. It's a gas-well building that I never go near. I
headed west for a quarter of a mile and turned for home,
feeling good. The pack turned with me, but I thought I
heard a barking dog off in the distance. I stopped to listen
but couldn't place it, so I decided the dog belonged to one of
the farms off in the distance. I was walking 38 free dogs that
day—no collars or leashes, but I have fairly good control
over them with distinct whistles and hand signals. Fairly
good, but not perfect, I should say.

I kept heading north, cross-country for home. One after
another, the dogs fell into place with me. Four of them had
their freshly caught lunch in their jaws, yummy gophers
that would be fought over once we get home. I spotted a
male coyote off to the west, pacing us with a bit too much
interest. He should have been loping away, not keeping even
with us, so I gave my special danger whistle. I only use this
tone of whistle when it is necessary to alert the pack. They
are supposed to come to me and fall in behind me as we
move out to a safer area or, in this case, home.

But then I stopped. From the sounds of it, one of my
dogs was trapped back in that buffalo pasture. She had
heard my danger whistle, and her yelps had intensified
loudly. She knew I wanted her with me. I turned, stood
still and listened. I told the pack to be quiet, and I listened
again. From the direction of that little building came a
frantic call for help. I was right—a dog really was trapped

127

somehow. I began to run. I was a runner with an old body stomped by broncs once too often, but I was running.

I came to the buffalo fence. The gas-well building was just on the other side, but I had sworn I would never enter a buffalo paddock again as long as I lived. Then I heard a dog yelping in apparent fear. I scaled that six-foot-high, steel fence—up it and down it. I called out and heard the dog yelp again. It was Jingles who was trapped under that measly building. I circled the building and watched two more dogs catch more gophers. They thought this was the best hunting day they'd had in years. Then I looked up and saw that the herd of buffalo had woken up from their siesta. In fact, they were ambling over the rise of the hill and breaking into a trot. In fact, they were now galloping, coming dead on, full out.

Regardless of my old body, I was over that fence so quick I should have won a medal for fence climbing. I stopped only long enough to give the danger whistle, and the pack fell in with me. I was still about three-quarters of a mile from home but made it back in record time, even after being forced to a more suitable walking pace.

I locked up the dogs in the yard and then it hit me: my four-by-four truck was at Fountain Tire for a bit of work. That left me with only my Ford Sable—a great car, but meant to be driven wisely on streets and highways, not across rough and rocky land. Nevertheless, I loaded the car with my six-foot-long, heavy steel crowbar, long-handled shovels, a flashlight to see under the building, and fresh water and a dish for the dog in distress. I added a few extras and was ready to go.

The car is a champion; after all it is a Ford. It plowed along where many four-by-four trucks would get stuck or die (did I mention it is 14 years old?). The car was feeling the pain but never quit. It is rough country, and this was no joy-ride. No streets, no highways, just rough pasture land with sinkholes, rocks and other hidden dangers. Most of the way, I took it slow and careful, although it was only by hitting the water at high speed that we made it through a slough without getting stuck or drowning out the motor.

The buffalo were gathered into a tight herd with heads up and their evil-looking curved horns glistening. In fact, they seemed to be very interested in the car. I had to come through the big steel swing gates into their pasture. All I wanted to do was bring a small car into their pasture. I wasn't going to enter on foot.

They crowded around, seeming happy to see the car. Maybe they thought it was a tractor coming with oats and other yummy feed. I tried threatening them in my meanest voice, "I am dangerous. I eat shaggy beasts like you, so run for your lives." They came closer. I tried throwing small pebbles at them, but they thought it was a game and gathered even closer. I didn't want to disappoint neighbours and others who think I like to get half-naked in broad daylight, so I ripped off my shirt and ran straight at the buffalo, whirling my shirt and hollering, "Shoo, you bad buffalo, shoo."

The herd turned as one body and ran. Now a fleet-footed runner, I charged back toward the big steel gate, opened it, quickly drove the car through the gate and then ran back breathlessly to close the gate before the buffalo got out. It was close, since they had turned in one body of fluid motion and were charging back. I was back in the safety of my poor car, which was sitting half in and half out of a clay-sucking mudhole.

I drove the short distance to the gas-well building, parked and got out. I heard pathetic cries for help coming from Jingles, who was trapped under the building. I was on a mission. Nothing would stop me from rescuing my dog. I parked the car alongside the building, then got out the flashlight and peered underneath it to ascertain my next steps. I saw the dog's frantically wagging tail as I lay on my side to peer at her. I hurt from laying on the hard-packed clay soil, but it didn't matter. I would rescue her.

As I lay on my side on the ground, with my poor quality, dollar-store flashlight, I glanced up. I had never seen such hairy legs. My gaze travelled up. "What hairy knees you have," I said to myself. Just about then, I felt the hot breath hit me on top of the head. I shifted position and gazed straight up into a buffalo's flared, intimidating nostrils. It had crept up and was standing literally over top of me. Even unshaven, my legs aren't that hairy. And even in the morning before brushing my teeth, my breath is not that hot and stinky. Being the brave person I am, I screamed insanely in panic and fear. The poor buffalo got hit in the head with my shriek of fear and jumped straight in the air in order to turn and run for its life. The thunder of hooves told me that the whole herd was running with her. I scrambled to my feet, my fear making my legs wobbly.

I was so shaken that I had trouble getting the crowbar and the long-handled shovel out of the back seat of the car to dig out my trapped dog. I found myself trembling so much that my teeth were chattering. I felt alone and so far from home. If anything bad happened to me, how many days would it be before anyone found me killed by a rampaging herd of buffalo? Would coyotes eat me out here on the lonely land as my trampled body lay roasting in the hot sun? Was this the end?

I hammered away at the solid clay ground with the crowbar. It was as hard as cement. I had to get to the wee beast and rescue her. Sweat trickled into my eyes. I had made a whopping two-inch-deep hole after an hour of chipping away at the ground. I thought of the jug of cool water I had brought for the trapped dog. Maybe I should have a sip of it. I turned toward the car, my thoughts on how many hours of daylight I had left to dig down and under to the dog.

And there sat my trapped, in-distress dog in the shade of the car, happily munching on the gopher she had gone under the building to get in the first place. Jingles smiled at me, grinning happily. While I was digging pathetically where she'd gone in, she had simply squeezed out of a narrow space on the other end of the building once she had caught her dinner. I didn't know whether to laugh or to cry. I chose to laugh, but not for long, because the herd of buffalo was trotting back toward me. Coming closer and closer! I boosted Jingles into the car, leaving her lunch behind. We beat a hasty retreat out of the pasture and headed for the quiet, rather boring life of home.

20

Lessons I Have Learned

LIFE IS LIKE A BOOK—first you're just a brand-new bundle of chubby cheeks and bare-bottomed joy. Like a newborn colt who is all big eyes and long legs. Like the beginning chapter of a new book on life. Pretty soon, you're up and about, toddling here and there like an inquisitive colt exploring its world in ever-widening circles away from the safety of its momma. The book of your life is now well started.

Then comes school age. Your mind is open to learning so many wonderful facts and figures. Sometimes you listen with every fibre in your body. Sometimes you resist because you don't want to learn today's lessons. Like you, the colt is now in training. He is learning the things he will need to know in order to be good at his job in the future. Those around you reading your book of life are fascinated by how quickly you're growing up.

Before your own momma is ready to release her maternal hold on you, you're off and running, all grown up and making your own way in life. The colt is now also well-educated and busy working for a living. Like you, he will have his days off to relax in the sun, and like you, he too will bend to the tasks at hand when called to.

Then comes the final chapter for all of us. And boy, do I ever have a few things to say after getting up there in age! Truthfully, I don't seem to know when I went from being a graceful filly to an old gray mare. But I do know I have learned a great many very interesting facts that I'd like to share with anyone with nothing better to do than listen.

Facts like what goes into a horse or dog must eventually exit the other end of said horse or dog. This fertilizer needs to be cleaned up on a regular basis. For the horses, this can be achieved by working the wrong end of a pitchfork. This hard, manual labour helps keep you in good physical shape in case anyone from a dating service ever wants to scrutinize your muscles.

For the dogs, I eventually tired of continually buying new pooper scoopers that got bent and twisted starting the day you ripped the price tag off them. So I drew up my own design, purchased the necessary equipment to build it and headed for the local welding shop in town. The man stopped

Life is never boring. Just give me a porch pony and a pooch and I am happy. MARGO MORTON

snickering about what I was building and got down to welding only after I rolled up my shirt sleeves to show him my heavily muscled arms from working that wrong end of a pitchfork one too many years. Then I stomped my feet just enough that he glanced down at the butt-kicking boots I was wearing. I guess he figured then that I was not someone to mess with. Now I have myself a pooper scooper that is indestructible. Made out of solid steel from the handle down. That puppy will still be around long after I am gone. No more bent, twisted store-bought stuff for me.

Another life lesson I've learned is that when things go wrong, they really, really go wrong. I do not believe in those old sayings that "bad luck comes in threes" or "three strikes and you're out." Because I can get my foot stomped by a horse very early in the morning (strike one), get bit by a cranky dog before noon (strike two), and try to go somewhere later on in the car and find out I have a flat tire with no spare (strike three). Now I think I'm safe for the rest of the day, only to have the same horse stomp on my foot during evening feeding, think the foot may be broken this time, hobble painfully to my truck to go to the hospital and then find out its battery is dead. Oh yeah, bad things come in more than threes, especially since I would have had that dog bite checked out at the same time.

But even though I know a lot at my advanced age, there are some things I haven't learned. Remember those koi I mentioned at the beginning of the book? The estimated price for an aquarium large enough for them was more than my whole house was worth. Being the resourceful type, I purchased a brand-spanking-new 200-gallon aluminum horse water tank and installed it on cinder blocks in my living room. The couch where I relaxed to watch the farmers' channel on my television had to be removed to make room. In fact, the matching rocking chair had to be removed too. I'm sure glad I don't watch much television.

In the spirit of things, I painted "Hillbilly Jacuzzi" in large letters on the side of my darling fishies' new home.

136

I had a lot of fun with a telephone repairman who had to enter my house to repair the phone line. He looked over at the lights, the bubbling water coming from below and the name on the tank and said, "You're kidding, right?"

I said, "Heck, no. That would be the day I'd pay that kind of money out for a fancy store-bought Jacuzzi. That's why I built my own, and it's darn nice to relax in it in the evening or on a lazy summer day." I then told him he was welcome to use it some evening if he wanted too. Free of charge, you know what I mean. Sadly, he declined. He was a good-looking fellow, too, better-looking than the pictures on that dating service.

The tank and paint were cheap enough, but the koi had other needs. I had to install a couple of pumps for cleaning their new home, and they needed certain timed lighting in order to keep growing year round. (I wanted them to grow huge, so no semi-hibernation for them during the winter months up here in northern Alberta.) And they were always starving. By the time everything was said and done, I could have built a pretty nice honeymoon shack in the spruce trees on my property in case any of those fellows from the dating service wanted to get to know me.

I have three koi, all metallic Ogons, all growing like . . . what? Fish? Ranger, my favourite, is smarter than a Jack Russell terrier and more devoted than a poodle. He will stand up partway out of the water to see what I am doing. Ranger loves to have his head petted, pressing his glistening orange noggin against my fingers. Koi can actually learn their names and do tricks, which Ranger enjoys doing on the days he has a mind to. As long as I feed him treats, he will swim though hoops and roll over just to earn his keep.

He and his buddies also can produce more manure than any horse I own. The cost of their food, pumps, filters, charcoal, medications and other necessities is more than I'd spend to properly care for a thousand-pound horse. Like I said at the start, I may never forgive my grandson Travis for getting me into this fish business.

I have to quit talking to you, as horses need to be fed, dogs need to be cared for and . . . good heavens, is that a skunk moseying across my lawn? Not again!

MARGO MORTON

About the Author

Gayle (Caskey) Bunney grew up in Oyen, Alberta, and has lived and worked with horses from the vast expanse of the southern prairies to the northwestern mountain regions with their forests and pristine beauty. She now resides in northeastern Alberta, near the town of Bonnyville. Here in this land of dense timber and numerous lakes and rivers, she is content in the natural splendour that surrounds her. Although now retired from owning horses, she continues to provide help and guidance to the many people who still turn to her daily for advice.

For the last several years, Gayle has surrounded herself with a pack of small-breed dogs that bring her great joy. As with horses, she is adept at caring for, grooming, breeding, training, doctoring and understanding the language and behaviour of her furry canine friends. Gayle is also a long-time rescuer of all types of animals and birds; she continues to learn everything she can about each living species. When asked how she manages to do so much for all the creatures in her care, she replies, "Humour, you have to have a sense of humour!"

Gayle is the author of three other books: *The Heart of a Horse, Horse Stories: Riding the Wind* and *My Life with Dogs*.

More Great Books in the Amazing Stories Series

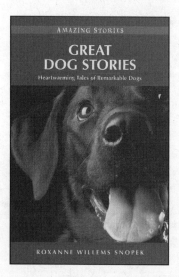

Great Dog Stories

Heartwarming Tales of Remarkable Dogs

Roxanne Willems Snopek

print ISBN 978-1-926613-97-0
ebook ISBN 978-1-926613-10-9

From small mixed-breed pets to devoted work partners performing life-saving duties, dogs are remarkable and versatile creatures that enrich our lives immeasurably. A service dog named Zephyr changes the life of celebrated children's author Jean Little. Mojo, an aging black Labrador retriever, gives the gift of courage to a cancer-stricken young boy. Eve, a sheepdog with a fear of sheep, becomes the first civilian-owned dog in Calgary to be certified as an RCMP Civilian Search and Rescue Dog. These inspiring tales of the love, dedication and intelligence of human-kind's canine companions are certain to be treasured by all animal lovers.

Visit heritagehouse.ca to see the entire list of books in this series.

More Great Books in the Amazing Stories Series

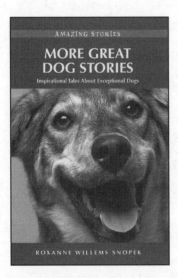

More Great Dog Stories

Inspirational Tales About Exceptional Dogs

Roxanne Willems Snopek

print ISBN 978-1-894974-57-8
ebook ISBN 978-1-926613-82-6

These are tales about people who turned around the lives of their dogs, and dogs who turned around the lives of their people. A retired greyhound named Blaster learns about life beyond the racetrack. Jovi, a fearful border collie, discovers the joys of human and canine companionship. A service dog named Blue opens doors for her owner, a quadriplegic, that he thought were forever closed to him. Dog lovers of all ages will be inspired and moved by these true stories.

Visit heritagehouse.ca to see the entire list of books in this series.

More Great Books in the Amazing Stories Series

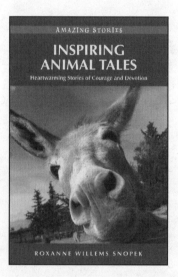

Inspiring Animal Tales

Heartwarming Stories of
Courage and Devotion

Roxanne Willems Snopek

print ISBN 978-1-894974-77-6
ebook ISBN 978-1-926936-22-2

Dogs, horses and other animals have long shown courage, trust and loyalty to the people in their lives, but they also inspire selfless love in return. This touching collection of true stories shows how people and animals come together to overcome life's challenges and find hope for the future. From National Service Dogs that give autistic children the gift of love and security to dedicated animal lovers who devote their lives to rescuing and healing abused or abandoned big cats, donkeys and parrots, the relationships portrayed in these stories are truly heartwarming.

Visit heritagehouse.ca to see the entire list of books in this series.

More Great Books in the Amazing Stories Series

Rescue Dogs

Crime and Rescue Canines
in the Canadian Rockies

Dale Portman

print ISBN 978-1-894974-78-3
ebook ISBN 978-1-926613-84-0

This dramatic collection of true stories by retired park warden Dale Portman tells how dogs became the silent heroes of search and rescue and law enforcement in the Canadian Rockies, beginning with Alfie Burstrom and his canine partner, Ginger, the first certified avalanche search team in North America. Working in severe weather and challenging terrain, dogs and their handlers save lives at the site of catastrophic avalanches, track missing persons and apprehend criminals. These stories of danger and devotion are sure to give readers a new appreciation of the vital role of working dogs in Canada's mountain parks.

Visit heritagehouse.ca to see the entire list of books in this series.

More Great Books in the Amazing Stories Series

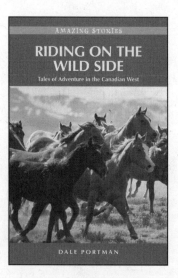

Riding on the Wild Side

Tales of Adventure in the Canadian West

Dale Portman

print ISBN 978-1-894974-80-6
ebook ISBN 978-1-926936-29-1

Park warden Dale Portman lived his dream of riding the range for a living in the spectacular Canadian Rockies. His exhilarating tales take us to an Old West world of wild horses and hair-raising roundups, youthful bravado and larger-than-life characters: Bert, the tough Millarville patriarch; Donny and Faye, free-spirited children of the Alberta foothills; and Jim, the eccentric English park warden who careens from one potential disaster to another. Filled with humour and adventure, these true stories capture the excitement and danger of backcountry life.

Visit heritagehouse.ca to see the entire list of books in this series.